£4

For Maria Shevtsova
with best wishes!
Wang Ning
Sept 30, 2006
Berlin

WANG NING

GLOBALIZATION AND CULTURAL TRANSLATION

MATERIALISING CHINA SERIES

Marshall Cavendish
Academic

© 2004 Marshall Cavendish International
(Singapore) Private Limited

Published 2004 by Marshall Cavendish Academic
An imprint of Marshall Cavendish International
(Singapore) Private Limited
A member of Times Publishing Limited

Times Centre, 1 New Industrial Road,
Singapore 536196
Tel:(65) 6213 9288
Fax: (65) 6284 9772
E-mail: mca@sg.marshallcavendish.com
Website:
http://www.marshallcavendish.com/academic

ISBN: 981-210-290-6

A CIP catalogue record for this book is available from
the National Library Board (Singapore).

Printed by Times Graphics Pte Ltd, Singapore
on non-acidic paper

**London • New York • Beijing • Shanghai
• Bangkok • Kuala Lumpur • Singapore**

MARSHALL CAVENDISH ACADEMIC

MATERIALISING CHINA: VISIONS AND PERSPECTIVES SERIES
Series Editors: Wang Ning and Ban Kah Choon

This series is intended for the reader interested in developments in key areas of Chinese society, culture, education, ideological systems, ethnicity, consumerism, and philosophical outlook. It focuses on social and economic developments as well as cultural and theoretical developments in contemporary China, and examines the manifestations, opportunities and contradictions of modernity, and the strategies put forward by China as it moves towards globalization. It also looks closely at the efforts to create an infrastructure both internally as well as internationally acceptable.

Other titles in the series

- Dismantling Time: Chinese Literature in the Age of Globalization *by Lu Jie*
- Cultural Studies in China *edited by Jin Yuanpu and Tao Dongfeng*
- Religious Studies in China *edited by Yang Huilin*
- Studies of Literature and Arts in China *edited by Fang Ning*
- Globalization and China *edited by Wang Ning*
- In Search of the Chinese Self-Identity *by Chen Yongguo*
- English and the Experience of Modernity *edited by Ban Kah Choon and Hu Zhuanglin*
- Translating China *by Luo Xuanmin*
- The Business of China: Doing Business and the Experience of China *edited by Xiao Guanglin and Shi Anbin*
- Multinational Corporations' Public Relations in China: An Interpretive Study of Public Relations Culture *by Liu Xi*
- Mediating *Chineseness*: Identity Politics and Media Culture in Contemporary China *by Shi Anbin*

About the Series Editors

WANG NING is Professor of English and Comparative Literature, and Director, Center for Comparative Literature and Cultural Studies, Tsinghua University, China.

BAN KAH CHOON is currently Visiting Professor, Mahidol University, Thailand, and was formerly Associate Professor of English Language and Literature, National University of Singapore.

Contents

Acknowledgements

The present book is the final result of my research project "Globalization and Cultural Translation", funded by the Center for Asian Studies, Tsinghua University. Without its generous support, I would not have been able to complete the manuscript in its present form.

Also, many of its chapters were originally written as individual essays and published either in international English journals or in a volume of selected conference papers. Although I had largely rewritten the earlier versions of these essays, I still want to express my heartfelt thanks to the following journals or presses, whose kind permissions have made it possible for me to rewrite them into the present book form.

Chapter 1 was originally published as "Globalization and Culture: the Chinese Cultural and Intellectual Strategy", *Neohelicon*, XXIX/ 2(2002): 101-114.

Chapter 2 was originally published as "Globalization, Cultural Studies and Translation Studies," *Translation Quarterly*, 15(2000), 37-50.

Chapter 3 was originally published as Globalizing Chinese Literature: Moving toward a Rewriting of Contemporary Chinese Literary Culture", *Journal of Contemporary China*, 13(38) (2004, February): 53-68.

Chapter 4 was originally published as "The Popularization of English and the 'Decolonization' of Chinese Critical Discourse", *ARIEL*, 31. 1/2 (2000): 412-424.

Chapter 6 was originally published as "Toward a Translation Study in the Context of Chinese-Western Comparative Culture Studies", *Perspectives: Studies in Translatology*, Vol. 4(1996): 43-52.

Chapter 7 was originally published as "Translating Theory: Toward a (Re)Construction of Chinese Critical Discourse", *ARIEL*, 34, forthcoming.

Chapter 8 was originally published as "Translation as Cultural '(De)Colonization'", *Perspectives: Studies in Translatology*, Vol. 10. 4(2002): 283-92.

Chapter 9 was originally published as "Cultural Studies in China: Towards Closing the Gap between Elite Culture and Popular Culture", *European Review* 11. 2(May 2003): 183-191.

Chapter 10 was originally published as "Whitman and Modernity in Regard to His Reception in Modern Chinese Literature", *Whitman East and West*, Ed Folsom ed., Iowa; University of Iowa Press, 2002, 197-207.

Chapter 11 was originally published as "Reconstructing Ibsen as an Artist: A Theoretical Reflection on the Reception of Ibsen in China", *Ibsen Studies* Vol. III, No. 1(2003):71-85.

Last but not least, thanks also go to my dear publishers and friends: Sim Khim Huang and Anthony E C Thomas, whose constant encouragement certainly helped me to finish this book within the given time. And Roy See's patient and careful editorial work has undoubtedly made the manuscript as close to perfect as possible before being published.

Wang Ning
Tsinghua University, Beijing
June 2004

CHAPTER 1

Globalization and Culture: The Chinese Cultural and Intellectual Strategy

In current cultural and academic circles, talking a lot about globalization has indeed become an academic fashion, which interests not only economists and politicians, but also intellectuals and scholars of the humanities and social sciences. It is not surprising to account for why so many people are talking about globalization in China: China's entry into the WTO has now come true and it has really involved itself in the process of globalization in an overall way. Also, because globalization concerns everybody's life and work, no one can ignore the objective existence of this ghost-like phenomenon. Undoubtedly, the advent of globalization in the current world is a contemporary event, especially in the Chinese context, but if we trace its origin in the West from an economic point of view, we find that it is by no means a twentieth-century event. As primarily an economic process that has lasted for over a hundred years, globalization has affected all aspects of contemporary life so rapidly that it is beyond people's expectation and resistance. So in the present chapter, I will first of all trace the origin of globalization before putting forward some positive and practical, cultural and intellectual strategies from the Chinese perspective toward its challenge.

THE MOVEMENT OF GLOBALIZATION: FROM THE WEST TO CHINA

Globalization is not something originating in Chinese soil, but rather something brought in from the West, like many of the high technologies and fashionable cultural and academic trends like modernism, postmodernism and postcolonialism. Here, I will first define our present age as that of globalization which manifests itself in various aspects. Just as William J. Martin describes, the world we live in is an "electronic global village where, through the mediation of information and communication technologies, new patterns of social and cultural organization are emerging".[1] In such an age of globalization, along with the fast floating of capital, both economic and cultural, and information, communication becomes more and more direct and convenient. The terrorist attacks in New York and Washington D.C. on 11 September 2001 appeared live immediately on the TV screen before hundreds of millions of TV viewers all over the world without difficulty due to the fast spread of information. This fact has undoubtedly changed the uncertain relations between China and the United States as well as the established world order and made people rethink any possible cultural conflicts between different nation-states. The compact state of time and space makes it possible for people at home to know everything that has happened in the world. It is true that globalization, especially in the humanities, is stubbornly resisted by the other strong force, localization, and various types of ethnicism or nationalism. We cannot but recognize that globalization is an objective phenomenon haunting our memory every now and then and influencing our cultural and intellectual life as well as our way of thinking and academic study. Under the impact of such a ghost-like globalization, the cultural and literary market has been shrinking, with elite culture being severely challenged by popular culture. The humanities and social sciences are severely challenged by the overload of knowledge and information. Transnational corporations have already transgressed the boundaries between nations, countries and even continents, where employees from different countries both work in the interests of their own countries as well as of their corporations. Different types of "agents" appear here and there, functioning both at the periphery and at the centre. It is predicted that in the age of globalization, the function of government will be replaced by this hidden "empire" in one way or another. So the empire "we are faced with wields enormous powers of oppression and destruction, but that fact should not make us nostalgic in any way for the old forms of domination. The passage to Empire and its processes of globalization offer new possibilities to the forces of liberation. Globalization, of course, is not one thing, and the multiple processes that we recognize as globalization are not unified or univocal. Our political task, we will argue, is not simply to resist these processes but to reorganize them and redirect them toward new ends. The creative forces of the multitude that sustain Empire are also capable of autonomously constructing a counter-Empire, and alternative political organization of global flows and exchanges".[2] Thus, in the age of globalization, all the artificial constructions of the centre have been deconstructed by the floating of capital and the new division of international labour. A new identity crisis has appeared in national cultures with the movement of the (Imperial) Western theory to the (peripheral) Orient and Third World countries. In the face of all this, we Chinese intellectuals cannot but raise such a question: What strategy should we adopt toward such a threatening challenge? Should we wait to be engulfed by the ghost-like globalization? Or should we still stubbornly resist this irresistible trend at the beginning of the new century?

In this sense, we might well predict that globalization is really a ghost-like spectre threatening our national mechanism, especially in the field of culture and literature. But things are not so simply defined. Naturally, in the face of all the above phenomena, we should first of all recognize that globalization gives rise to the interpenetrating processes of the universalization of particularism and the particularization of universalism.[3] That is, the impact of globalization is embodied at two different poles: Its effect travels from the West to the East and, at the same time, from the East to the West. Or as Fredric Jameson points out, "We have in this particular instance observed the endowment of the abstract of opposition of Identity and Difference with a specific content of unity versus multiplicity."[4] Marxist dialectical materialism has taught us not to limit ourselves to the one-sidedness of anything. The process of globalization is always juxtaposed with that of localization. Where there is the power of globalization, there is the existing force of localization. Only in this way can our present world always be in a state of development. Since globalization is a rather complicated phenomenon, I will first of all look upon it as a process that started long before the latter part of the twentieth century. And in this aspect, it is worth re-reading what Marx and Engels described more than one-and-a-half centuries ago in their monumental *Communist Manifesto*: The discovery of America has undoubtedly enabled capitalism to expand its influence worldwide, along with the start of a sort of travelling capital, which culminated in the latter part of the twentieth century. It is not only true of material production, but also true of cultural production: "And as in material, so also in intellectual production. The intellectual creations of individual nations become common property. National one-sidedness and narrow-mindedness become more and more impossible, and from the numerous national and local literatures, there arises a world literature."[5] Here, to my understanding, the so-called "world literature" does not mean one homogenized type of literature, but rather a sort of general literary trend of diverse orientation. Unlike what happens in the field of economy, the globalization of culture can by no means bring about only one type of culture, which will develop at any time in a pluralistic orientation.

Thus, we can clearly see, after a careful reading of the above quotation in *Communist Manifesto*, that Marx and Engels have at least touched upon four issues which are very relevant to our study of globalization in today's cultural and intellectual context: (1) the origin of economic globalization and the process of its movement from the West to the East; (2) the division of international labour caused by the rise of capitalism and the consequent accumulation and expansion of capital; (3) the emergence of transnational capitalization, the floating of funds and the formation of transnational corporations; and (4) the intellectual production brought about by material production and the appearance of a sort of world literature. It should be pointed out that the later rise of comparative literature as a new discipline in the latter part of the nineteenth century has undoubtedly proved the prophecy made by Marx and Engels. In this sense, whether we deal with economic globalization or cultural globalization, we cannot but find the internal linkage between the two, and some inspiration and resources from the Marxist doctrine. Although Marx and Engels do not directly deal with the relationship between (economic) globalization, (cultural) production and aesthetic representation, they have actually touched upon the fact that cultural and intellectual production is also caused and affected by the process of economic globalization. As Marxists ourselves, we cannot deliberately separate culture from economy as the two are more and more closely related in the current age of globalization.

Although I do not agree with the "homogenizing" practice of cultural globalization, we cannot neglect the increasing homogenizing tendency of contemporary culture, with strong (First World) cultures penetrating weak (Third World) cultures more and more. Cultural communication always occurs like this: the communication of strong cultures influencing and penetrating weak cultures. In this sense, I would rather refer to Jameson's insightful idea about the linkage between

4

globalization and culture: "I believe that globalization is a communicational concept, which alternately masks and transmits cultural or economic meanings. We have a sense that there are denser and more extensive communicational networks all over the world today, networks that are on the one hand the result of remarkable innovations in communicational technologies of all kinds, and on the other have as their foundation the tendentially greater degree of modernization in all the countries of the world, or at least in their big cities, which includes the implantation of such technologies."[6] As one of the few eminent contemporary Marxist theorists in the West, Jameson's words actually tell us that the globalization of culture is carried out largely by means of the communication of information, another form of cultural translation. Since our age is also known as an age of information, the spreading and floating of information cannot but influence the production of culture and its elite form—literature and art. So in the next section, I will deal with the current situation of literature and culture in China being influenced by the advent of globalization and the rise of its consequence—popular culture or consumer culture—which has already been threatening the existence of elite culture and its product—literature and art.

REFLECTIONS ON THE CURRENT CHINESE LITERARY AND CULTURAL SITUATION

Obviously, the impact of globalization on literary and cultural production and representation is so deep that it is beyond anyone's expectation and resistance. Since I am a Chinese scholar doing both literary and cultural studies, I will, in this section, focus on the current Chinese literary and cultural situation as I think it might prove the internal and external connections between globalization and literature and culture in the present time. As such, it is necessary to observe the case of contemporary Chinese society first. Since the beginning of the 1990s, China has been involved in the process of creating a market economy in a broader context of global and transnational capitalization, which cannot but have affected our studies of culture and literature. The Chinese government has always maintained the strategy that, politically, it should always take the road of socialism, or a sort of socialism of "Chinese characteristics", but on the other hand, it does welcome foreign investment if it can be limited to the domain of the economy and finances without influencing Chinese political

5

and cultural policy. Actually, we cannot avoid the fact that the investment of foreign capital will influence the production of literature and culture. In the face of the strong impact of the market economy as a direct consequence of economic globalization, consumer culture has become one of the hot topics confronting Chinese scholars of both literary and cultural studies. The culture which is characterized by being manufactured, commercial and consumptive undoubtedly destroys the elegance and sublimity of elite culture and its products, literature and art. The attempt to redefine culture appears now and then in some scholarly books of humanistic spirit, but the attention given to consumer culture in China is strikingly different from the great importance attached to it in Western academic circles. Popular culture or consumer culture has always been severely criticized as something unhealthy and something that rebels against the traditional humanistic spirit in current Chinese critical circles.[7] But ironically speaking, popular culture or consumer culture has indeed permeated our daily life and even academic research and cultural production, challenging our elite and canonical sense of literature and art. Scholars of literature and art cannot but be confronted with such questions: How should we face the severe challenge raised by the rise of popular culture? What will be the future of canonical literature and art in the age of globalization when information is spreading very swiftly and across boundaries? Should we still maintain the binary opposition between elite culture and popular culture in such an age of globalization when the situation is more favourable for the production of popular culture and literature, as these are more welcomed by the broad masses of people?

As we all know, exploring consumer culture in the West was not a unique event at all in the 1990s. Early in the discussion on postmodernism launched in the circles of American culture and literary theory, quite a few critics had already touched upon consumer culture in the post-industrial society in an attempt to "cross the border" between high culture and low culture and "close the gap" between canonical literature and popular literature. Leslie Fiedler and many others, standing at the forefront of defending the legitimacy of popular culture, once tried to narrow the artificial gap between elite culture and popular culture. He sharply points out: "It is time, at any rate, to be through with pretense; for to Close the Gap means also to Cross the Border between the Marvelous and the Probable, the Real and the Mythical, the world of the boudoir and the counting house and the realm of what

6

used to be called Faerie, but has for so long been designated mere madness. Certainly the basic images of Pop forms like the Western, Science Fiction and Pornography suggest mythological as well as political or metapolitical meanings."[8]

Apparently, even at the time, Fiedler's effort already points to the other aspect of postmodernism: its merging into contemporary popular culture and even consumer culture. His insightful observation actually anticipated the later study and critique of postmodernism made by Jameson and other Marxist critics. It also paved the way more or less for the later rise of cultural criticism and cultural studies in North American academic circles, which deal in a theoretical way with popular culture and consumer culture. To Fiedler, the difference between postmodernism and modernism lies in its crossing the artificial border between elite culture and popular culture and closing the natural gap between elite literature and popular literature. The reason why the modernist elite culture is severely challenged in the contemporary era is simply because it confines itself to the isolated ivory tower—it is incompatible with the broad masses of audience (consumers of culture and art), and is hardly able to escape the unfavourable situation. Postmodernism, however, tries in a flexible way to bridge the gap between high culture and popular culture tactfully. But because it is decentralization- and plurality-oriented, postmodernism would bring about an obscure and relative standard with which to judge the value of art. As a result, duplicated art and pastiched art appear, made with high technology and characterized by depthlessness, plainness, multiplicity, collage and fragmentariness. In the postmodern age, those high cultural products and works of art are seen as consumer goods: Unrestrained duplication, parody, multiplication and even wholesale manufacture have replaced elaborate works of art in the modernist age; plain characterization has replaced the profound analysis of characters' psychological description; and fragmentary or even schizophrenic structure has replaced the modernist depth structure, etc. The appearance of all the above has certainly attracted the attention of scholars and theorists who have a strong social responsibility, but their concern does not merely lie in their opposition to these phenomena, but rather in their effort to confront these complicated phenomena so as to anatomize them from the perspective of cultural studies. Through these analyses and interpretations, they could probably offer some practical strategies. I think of it as a positive attitude, the result of which will not intensify the established opposition between the two types of culture but will help them to co-exist and complement each other. In this way, their relations should not be "either/or" but rather "both/and". This is perhaps the revelation that postmodernism could bring to us. Actually, unlike the ambitious doctrine of enlightening people practised by the modernists, the doctrine adopted by the postmodernists tries to enlighten people in a different way by identifying itself first with popular culture, in the process of raising the level of popular culture. This is probably the so-called "post-enlightenment" doctrine which is characterized by not only narrowing the gap between the two types of culture but also enabling communication and dialogue between them.

In the current Chinese cultural and intellectual context, some humanities scholars and critics are very much worried about the prevalence of consumer culture and art in recent years, trying to oppose its challenge by hopelessly "saving the crisis of the humanistic spirit".[9] This is not hard to imagine. But consequently, it might well intensify the existing opposition between elite culture and popular culture. In a society where the market economy is gradually becoming dominant according to the laws and regulations of the WTO, such opposition will undoubtedly lead to the death of elite culture and art if it is distanced from the broad masses of people. The fact is that consumer culture does occupy an important place in contemporary China, dominating cultural production and communication like a hidden God. So if we realize the legitimacy of its existence and make proper use of it, it would probably help produce high cultural products; otherwise, it would gradually swallow the already shrinking cultural market. Along with China's recent entry into the WTO, this consequence will become clearer to us scholars of the humanities and social sciences. The government-dominant society will be replaced by a market-dominant society where the function of the government will be less and less important. So at the moment, both the government officials and quite a few scholars are thinking of some practical strategies to counter the possible challenge created by the laws and regulations of the WTO. Since China's contemporary cultural production is closely related to the economy, it is also necessary for us to be aware of what cultural studies are going on in the West or elsewhere.

Since the beginning of the 1990s, China's socialist-plan economy has been shifting toward a market economy, and the country has been in transition with respect to politics, economics and culture, with different forces and discourses co-existing and complementing each other. Some scholars are still exploring cultural theory proper and its value in the academic circles, with the objective of a conscious construction of Chinese cultural theory;[10] international cultural exchanges have made it possible for Chinese–Western academic communication and theoretical dialogue to take place; the production of high cultural products in the form of literature and art occurs under the conditions of a market economy, with the *avant-garde* productions fading away; and the rise of consumer culture, which is developing in a pluralistically oriented direction, challenges traditional elite culture and the humanities. But on the other hand, some publishing houses still try to publish excellent canonical literary works in perfectly designed form; that is, serious literature and art can still be produced in a popular way, but the effect is not always conspicuous. In light of all this, what strategy should we adopt? I think that the scholars of cultural studies in contemporary China have really done something practical. So it is necessary here to summarize briefly the positive impacts of the introduction of cultural studies since the beginning of the 1990s.

Cultural studies, as a newly rising branch of learning and an interdisciplinary discourse, was first introduced in China at the beginning of the 1990s, with such journals as *Dushu* (Reading), *Guowai wenxue* (Foreign Literatures), *Wenyi yanjiu* (Literature and Art Studies), *Wenxue pinglun* (Literary Review) and *Tongsu wenxue pinglun* (Review of Popular Literature) enthusiastically pushing forward its development in the Chinese context. One of the culminating achievements made in China's cultural studies, from an international point of view, was the International Conference on Cultural Studies: China and the West, held in Dalian in August 1995. Such international scholars in this field as Ralph Cohen, Terry Eagleton and Jonathan Arac attended the conference. As a result, a special issue was put up in the internationally prestigious journal, *New Literary History*, which presented the state of the art of cultural studies in China before the international scholarship.[11] Another milestone in China's cultural studies was the publication of the journal, *Wenhua yanjiu* (Cultural Studies), in Tianjin at the beginning of the twenty-first century.[12] With the joint efforts made by literary scholars, sociologists, anthropologists and communication scholars, cultural studies has become a very promising new discipline in China and a dynamic critical discourse which will help restructure the established university curriculum and division of traditional disciplines and branches of learning. Unlike its opposition to comparative literature in Western academic circles, its practice has proved that it can at least co-exist with literary studies, especially with a cross-cultural study of Chinese–Western comparative literature.[13]

GLOBAL, LOCAL OR "GLOBAL IN THE LOCAL"?

In the current debate on globalization and culture in the Chinese context, exploring the relations between globalization and culture is becoming more and more attractive to both literary and cultural studies scholarship. In this aspect, American scholar Arif Dirlik is largely quoted as he has published extensively both in English and in Chinese, and he frequently visits China giving lectures and speeches in different universities.[14] One of his famous strategies is the so-called "global/local" strategy. That is, globalization can only be realized in the local context, for the practice of globalization in any place should be restricted to the local force. That is very much like the saying "think globally and act locally". Actually, according to Dirlik, "from the perspective of global capitalism, the local is a site of liberation but manipulation; stated differently, it is a site the inhabitants of which must be liberated from themselves (stripped of their identity) to be homogenized into the global culture of capital (their identities reconstructed accordingly). Ironically, even as it seeks to homogenize populations globally, consuming their cultures, global capitalism enhances awareness of the local, pointing to it also as the site of resistance to capital".[15] Since we live in an age of globalization, we cannot but be in such a process of global economization and transnational capitalization as China is already a member of the WTO. And in this globalizing process, everybody should be more or less restricted to the cruel "law of jungle". Obviously, globalization has marginalized most people politically, economically and even culturally. It is especially true of those intellectuals of the humanities whose research achievements cannot necessarily be evaluated by immediate economic profits: The shrinking of the cultural market and the cutting of research funds and even corporatization of departments in universities are all the ruthless facts confronting us. So it is not surprising that it is resisted by another strong and stubborn force—localization—which finds particular embodiment in the fields of social science and the humanities.

Currently in China as well as in some other Asian countries, the revival of Confucianism might well serve as an oppositional force against the challenge of globalization. In this context, some Asian intellectuals have been trying to search for an Asian national and cultural identity, which is undoubtedly an Asian version of postcolonialism.[16] Paradoxically, China does not prevent economic globalization from affecting the country, for it might well help to stimulate the rapid development of the Chinese economy; but culturally, it does try to prevent its culture from being "globalized" or "homogenized", which finds particular embodiment in the significant respect shown to Confucius, the symbol of its tradition, who was severely castigated during the May 4th period and later in the Cultural Revolution.[17] For, to many people, to be modernized simply means to be Westernized, or more exactly, colonized. Since Chinese culture should undergo its demarginalization from the periphery to the centre, its first step should be to "decolonize" itself in the "homogenizing" context of globalization.

In this way, even to many Chinese intellectuals, if it is almost impossible to oppose economic globalization, then cultural globalization will most probably be resisted or at least slowed down. In some sense, cultural globalization, as a direct consequence of economic globalization, is also a result of the international postmodern cultural movement. Faced with the impact of Western postmodernism, contemporary Chinese consumer culture marked with various types of "postmodernism" or "quasi-postmodernism" manifests itself in different forms: The weekly supplements of various newspapers have become a sort of "cultural snack"; TV programmes which have attracted a wider audience pose a strong challenge to the film industry, which needs greater investment and more advanced technology, thus confronting Chinese cinema with a double challenge—that from Hollywood (Western culture) and from the local environment (mass media and consumer culture); the discotheques and popular songs degrade serious music; the joint operations of discourse, power and the market economy restrict the development of the book market; and the development of high technology and advanced duplicating techniques in the post-industrial age has made it possible for popular singers and film stars to be trained and become well-known in the form of MTV, etc. It is true that cultural producers have already clearly realized and seriously considered the impact of "consumers" (readers and audiences) in the process of creating cultural products and works of art, which is obviously a great improvement as compared to the past when the government presided over the production of all cultural and literary works.[18] But cultural product cannot be equated with the production of consumables. Its value cannot be judged according to its reception in the market and the quantity of production. From a long-term point of view, cultural production should be juxtaposed with the development of a country's economy.

Apparently, in the age of globalization, postmodernism should be, and actually has been, more or less redefined in regard to its critical and creative reception in some Oriental and Third World countries: It originated in the Western cultural soil, then swept over Europe and other regions, and has finally become a global phenomenon, which has resulted in cultural globalization at present. Just as Jameson points out in discussing the reception of postmodernism in China, apart from the Western influence and Chinese scholars' conscious introduction to and creative reception of postmodernism, its prevalence and the appearance of the various facets of postmodernity in China and other places also depend on three other factors: the operation of transnational funds, global capitalization and the advent of cyberspace.[19] These three factors, especially the rapidly developing media industry, together form a powerful force pushing the process of cultural globalization forward, moving it from the centre to the periphery and functioning both at the centre and at the periphery. Even the strongest mechanism of national culture cannot resist this force. However, postmodernism or postmodernity does not always bring about negative impacts. It has broken through our one-dimensional mode of thinking, making our reflections on the problems of the age more sophisticated and our pursuit of value standards beyond the "either/or" mode of thinking. Therefore, according to Jameson, "in the most interesting postmodernist works, however, one can detect a more positive conception of relationship, which restores its proper tension to the notion of difference itself. This new mode of relationship through difference may sometimes be an achieved new and original way of thinking and perceiving; more often it takes the form of an impossible imperative to achieve that new mutation in what can perhaps no longer be called consciousness".[20] Now that the plurality-oriented mode of thinking can endow us with an endless spirit of exploration, we should try to turn the unfavourable into the favourable in this new condition. Only in this way can we do our work better.

Now globalization has also influenced the establishment of China's national and cultural identity. Whether we like it or not, we cannot but be involved in such a powerful process. Economic and financial globalization has undoubtedly brought about good opportunities for China to catch up with and even surpass the advanced Western countries, thus involving China in the world economic stage as early as possible. It has also challenged the existence of quite a number of state-owned enterprises, resulting in unemployment and hardship for many laid-off workers. What we intellectuals are most concerned about is the spread and the threatening power of a sort of cultural globalization on which we must focus our attention. Despite the fact that cultural globalization may easily blur the national and cultural identity of an individual national culture, it can still bring about something positive. It brings us both positive and negative effects, that is to say, both challenge and opportunity. If we face the challenge in a critical way and make full use of the opportunity to develop our national culture in a broad international context, we will most probably highlight the Chinese national and cultural identity and create an awareness of the essence of Chinese culture in the international community. In this sense, stubbornly resisting this trend by taking a postcolonial stand will only lead to further conflict between China and the West. Undoubtedly, as Third World intellectuals, we have perceived the impact of this current trend on our national culture to various degrees, which puzzles some of us. For instance, a conspicuous oppositional strategy would be to put forward the concept of Third World culture and localism, a metamorphosed version of postcolonialism,[21] which not only prevails in the mainland of China, but in Hong Kong, Taiwan and other overseas Chinese communities. This raises an inevitable question: Is it really necessary to set up such a binary opposition as that between globalization and localization? I myself, as well as quite a few other intellectuals, do not want to see such artificial opposition, but how should we transcend such binary opposition so as to achieve equitable dialogue between the Chinese and international scholarship?

Obviously, there are two kinds of postcoloniality in current China and although it was never a totally colonized country in the past, China's successful take-over of its former colonial regions, Hong Kong (on 1 July 1997) and Macau (in December 1999), has certainly proved that China has made great advances in the process of postmodernization and global decolonization. Thus, postmodernity and postcoloniality are inseparably relevant to each other as a direct consequence of cultural globalization. It is true that many of the contemporary Western postmodern and postcolonial scholars are interested in Oriental and Third World culture. In recognizing the unique value of non-Western culture, they try to discover something which might well help them get out of the "crisis of representation". Jameson once tried to prove through his reading of Lu Xun's "The True Story of Ah Q" (*Ah Q zheng zhuan*) that all the Third World literary texts could be read as certain national allegories.[22] Edward Said, who has an Oriental background, also admits,

"I am very interested in Third World literature. In many of the gestures made by writers, but not all certainly, there's a quite conscious effort to re-do and re-absorb the canon in some way."[23] They strive to undermine and even deconstruct at the very centre of the Imperial empire its cultural and linguistic hegemony, struggling for the First World intellectuals to know about the Third World better. As scholars of the Third World, we highly appreciate their critique of the Western Imperial empire and its hegemonism. But unfortunately, some Western people might well regard China as a potential threat as it has in recent years been developing so rapidly in its economy. This unnecessary worry is really misleading.[24]

Actually, in current Chinese society, things are different. On the one hand, China's openness to the outside world and economic reform in the past decades have made its economy rise rapidly, but on the other hand, as China is vast in terms of space and population, it always develops in an uneven way, with different elements of the "primitive", "premodern", "modern" and "postmodern" mixed up in the same country. In such a large country, anything contingent could happen beyond one's expectation. In evaluating Gilles Deleuze's potential influence in the twentieth century, Michel Foucault once raised this meaningful question: "Will this century be known as Deleuzian?" If we think it appropriate to describe the political and cultural situation in the West since the latter part of the 1960s as Deleuzian, it is even truer of the current Chinese situation at the beginning of the new century. Undoubtedly, the consequence of postmodernity in China has also helped re-periodize Chinese culture and literature after 1978, as reflected in the New Period (*Xin shiqi*) and the Post-New Period (*Hou xin shiqi*). The former is characterized by a political event and the latter by a form of cultural politics known as cultural transformation, which, to some extent, results from the international postmodernist movement and cultural globalization.[25] Thus, Chinese postmodernity manifests itself in a way that is becoming more closely related to the global postcolonial movement, which finds particular embodiment in the following two aspects: Domestically, it is not only effective in undermining the power of the master narrative, but also in deconstructing the dominance of the official discourse, which is marked by the rise of popular culture and even consumer culture and literature. Internationally, the practice of, or the debate on, Chinese postmodernity in the Post-New Period has indeed helped its de-territorializing or decentralizing attempt to move from the periphery to the centre, thus creating a pluralistic centre rather than merely a monolithic "West-centric" one.

In view of the above observations, I hold that we particularly need stable external surroundings for China's modernizations, especially in the present age of globalization. Culturally and theoretically speaking, observing and analyzing the phenomenon of globalization will help us to objectively evaluate the "forces of globalization" from the perspective of "travelling theory". If critical theory can spread as far as to a remote country, what about globalization? In my view, we would rather use this term in an opposite way, that is, we could globalize Oriental and Chinese culture in the world in such an age of globalization. And in this sense, we ought to have more communication and dialogue with the international community rather than maintain an oppositional attitude toward the West.[26] Since globalization is an issue heatedly discussed and debated internationally, we should have direct dialogue with our international colleagues, even in the English language, which is no longer merely a Western language but rather an international language, for through communication and dialogue, we can at least know the state of the art in the study of this field. We know clearly that preserving some characteristics of national identity is certainly necessary, but any attempt to over-emphasize localization at the expense of excluding foreign influence will easily give rise to an inadequate nationalist sentiment and result in an unfavourable condition for China's stable external surroundings. In the current face of cultural globalization, we Chinese intellectuals should have this practical strategy: First of all, conform to it without sacrificing our national and cultural identity, and then expand our cultural communication and academic dialogue with the international community rather than just with Western academic circles. Since China is a large country with a splendid cultural heritage, it ought to make greater contributions to world civilizations and the construction of world culture not only economically but also culturally and intellectually. Chinese intellectuals should form a strong voice in the international forum and have equitable dialogue with the international scholarship.

CHAPTER 2

Globalization, Cultural Studies and Translation Studies

Translation studies, as a sub-discipline of the humanities and social sciences, has recently changed its focus of attention, from previous attention only to the text to the present greater concern for the context. This phenomenon has undoubtedly been influenced by the current prevailing trend of cultural studies in the era known as that of globalization. To deal with issues in translation studies, it is necessary first of all to approach the issue of globalization and cultural studies.

GLOBALIZING TRANSLATION STUDIES IN THE CONTEXT OF CULTURAL STUDIES

Globalization, like other Western concepts, has finally arrived in China, exercising a strong influence on China's economy and finances. This time, this phenomenon does not merely function culturally and academically, but rather economically and financially, posing a serious challenge to those engaged in the study of humanities and social sciences. Its advent has obviously marginalized more than 80 per cent of the Chinese people, with less than 20 per cent directly benefiting from it. China has to make its own choice—although it is reluctant to do so—whether to involve itself in this worldwide historical trend or resist it with its own national mechanism. Obviously, it has adopted the former attitude since it intends to position itself in the intense worldwide economic competition to develop its national economy. As a direct consequence of economic globalization, scholars of both the humanities and social sciences have been increasingly confronted by cultural globalization. Although many of my colleagues are opposed to the process of cultural globalization, I still think it is necessary to adopt a dialectical attitude toward such a phenomenon. That is, cultural globalization will certainly bring us both negative and positive results. Its positive aspect lies in the fact that it enables our cultural industry and academic research to be manipulated according to the rules of the market economy rather than by the previous government's political interventions, thereby linking economic construction to cultural construction more closely, while its negative aspect obviously lies in making the production of elite culture or non-market-oriented cultural production more and more difficult, as a result of which a new sort of hierarchy is formed. But even when confronted with this kind of impact, we can still readjust the inter-relations between globalization and cultural construction. What we should do at the moment is to first of all conform to the trend of globalization before using it to spread the influence of Chinese culture in the world without doing harm to our national cultural identity. Thus, it is quite reasonable to attach great importance to translation as well as translation studies since translation must play a vital role in intercultural communication in the context of globalization.

Since translation always stands between at least two languages and cultures, its critical function has thus manifested itself more evidently. In the present age of globalization, translation plays an increasingly important role in international communication, especially in English–Chinese translation and vice versa, with the Internet becoming more and more popular in the non-English-speaking world. Translation studies, as a comparatively independent branch of learning dealing with issues of intercultural communication and translation, should also be globalized, for it has already appeared in cultural studies not only in the West but recently in China; thus, a drastic change of focus has taken place in translation studies in China.

In the current world of Chinese culture and academia, especially in the field of literary theory and criticism, talking a lot about cultural studies has become a fashion, especially since the beginning of the 1990s after the critical response to the international post modernism debate. Undoubtedly, doing translation studies without referring to cultural studies will not work as translation is now regarded firstly as an intercultural action. So it is not surprising that scholars devoted to traditional cultural studies or critics dealing with contemporary cultural criticism are exclusively interested in this heatedly debated issue in the West and are even trying to apply contemporary Western cultural theory in the interpretation of some practical Chinese cultural phenomena. Similarly, in the long-marginalized sphere of translation studies, there

17

are some scholars both at home and abroad who have tried to replace traditional literal translation with cultural translation and interpretation.[1] This is a good beginning to me, for in my view, translation studies comprises at least two elements: In a narrower sense, it deals with literal translation aimed at converting the content in one language into another language; and in a broader sense, it explores the changing of the cultural connotation in the source language into another cultural form in the target language. The former is called literal translation and the latter, cultural translation. Literal translation is, to a large extent, restricted by the yoke of linguistic form, while cultural translation is more open to dynamic interpretation and cultural representation. At the moment, along with the impact of cultural studies, translation studies is gaining a more cultural and theoretical orientation. The action of translation is first viewed as an action of cultural communication, and then cultural interpretation. It cannot take place without associating itself with culture. But in view of the state of the art of the research on translation in China in general, there are only a few scholars who are involved in translation studies from the perspective of cultural studies. Due to their limited knowledge of recent developments in Western translation studies in the broad context of cultural studies, many translation scholars would rather stick to technical operation and value judgement than enlarge the connotation of translation to encompass the aspect of culture. Since I myself have been engaged in literary and cultural criticism and studies, I am more interested in exploring some relevant issues concerning translation studies in such an intercultural context.

REDEFINING TRANSLATION IN THE CONTEXT OF CULTURAL STUDIES

As both literal translation and cultural translation are associated with two cultural contexts in which the cultural content is conveyed in two different languages, these two types of translation can both be regarded as cultural translation in its narrow sense as well as in its broad sense. Undoubtedly, one of the basic principles of translation is that the translated version should be faithful to the original; namely, reaching the plane of the so-called "*xin*" ("faithfulness") as defined by Yan Fu a hundred years ago and heatedly debated in the field of Chinese translation studies for almost a century. According to this principle, the translation should first of all be faithful to the content of the original, with literal translation laying more emphasis on formal fidelity, and cultural translation laying more emphasis on how to convey in a precise way the original cultural connotation and how to interpret it or even rewrite it more or less on the basis of the native cultural background. Both approaches can reach the plane of faithfulness in varying degrees, with literal translation on the level of linguistic fidelity and cultural translation on that of cultural faithfulness. Thus, these two types of translation are similar to a large extent. How, then, should we handle the dialectical relations between the two? This, to me, is the very issue that current translation studies must confront. I once affirmed elsewhere that we did not have translation studies in China in its real sense which could make it possible for translators to carry out dialogues with our Western colleagues or with the international translation scholarship, and that what we did have was only translation criticism and translation review, which is necessary to our teaching and practical use of translation. That is to say, those dealing with translation criticism are largely confined to endless technical analysis and the shallow value judgement of translation practice, with their conclusions more empirical than theoretical and far from academic research and theoretical construction. Of course, such research results could be more or less useful to practising translators in their teaching and translation practice, but they cannot be theorized into academic advances and globalized as universally applicable guiding principles. It may be one of the reasons why translation studies, as a comparatively independent branch of learning in China, has long been neglected or even intentionally marginalized.[2] I still hold this view now, but in recent years, with the joint efforts made by my colleagues, things have been largely improved; China's translation studies have certainly taken a new step in the direction of the international level of scholarship.[3] International conferences on translation studies have been held in China, and quite a few Chinese scholars frequently attend conferences abroad and publish their essays in international journals.[4] All this indicates that Chinese translation studies is now beginning to move from its original periphery to the academic centre in an attempt to engage in equitable dialogue with the international translation scholarship.

Since Chinese culture and Western culture have entirely different traditions, each is more or less "mysterious" to the other. It is true, according to Eugene Eoyang, that such a "mysteriousness" has been in existence for quite a long time: "In surveying the history of translation, one encounters so many traditional misconceptions, shibboleths, and half-truths that no systematic analysis is possible before these 'weeds' of confusion are cleared away. Yet these 'errancies' are not blatant 'vulgar' errors, for they cannot be accurately characterized as weeds to be cleared away or destroyed, since each of them contains a kernel of truth that must be recognized. It is for this reason I call these anomalies 'myths' rather than errors, because 'error' would presuppose a prior original 'truth' that is contravened."[5] Obviously, it is from the cultural perspective that the above conclusion is arrived at since Eoyang himself is an "intercultural" scholar or a Chinese–Western comparatist. But if we want to communicate with our Western colleagues on a level plane, how can we overcome the impediment of such a "myth"? To me, we should neither cater to the taste of Western scholars nor express our own view without paying any attention to the Western audience, for neither of these approaches will lead to real dialogues. What we should do is to find a topic which is of common interest and which will give rise to theoretical discussion and even debate in our intercultural comparative studies. In this way, the dialogue will be of certain significance. At present, what kind of topic will enable Chinese and Western scholars to have dialogues on the issues concerning translation studies? Can we find a way to transcend the barriers of language and academic discourse? Judging from the present scholarly interest both in China and in the West, I think cultural studies might well function as the common ground on which we can break through the yoke of the prison-house of language in our cross-cultural communication and academic dialogue.

As far as the so-called cultural studies is concerned, one would immediately think of the cultural studies prevailing in Western cultural and critical circles. It obviously does not mean elite culture in its traditional sense, but refers rather to the study of contemporary culture and even popular culture, including studies of such topics as ethnicity, gender, race, consumer culture and the mass media. The rise of cultural studies has undoubtedly paved the way for all the marginalized discourses to challenge elite culture, thus realizing its objective of moving from the periphery to the centre and functioning both at the periphery and at the centre. Hence, translation studies as a means of cultural and literary communication should be included in cultural studies, which actually functions as an umbrella covering all aspects of contemporary cultural and intellectual life. It is in effect an interdisciplinary and intercultural branch of learning prevailing in current Western academic circles and, in recent years, cultural studies has also been playing a more and more dominant role in Chinese intellectual life, especially in Hong Kong and Taiwan. As is well-known, cultural studies first originated in the British literary research field in the 1950s, with F. R. Leavis as its representative. At the time, cultural studies was only characterized by cultural criticism of literary phenomena, with a strong elite sense of enlightenment. In the face of the impact of some subaltern discourses, there have appeared pluralistically oriented directions within the domain of cultural studies, with one direction gradually heading out of the earlier sphere of canonical study of literature and including studies of society and community life and even the mass media, thereby converging into the mainstream of contemporary cultural studies. As cultural studies is more concerned about contemporary and non-elite culture or, more specifically, popular culture and mass media, it should not exclude translation studies since translation itself is always regarded as a means of cultural and literary communication. As far as its basic definition is concerned, the major task in translation is to convert the cultural content in one language into another, so whether the translation is faithful or not largely depends on the extent of the translator's grasp of the two languages, both in form and in spirit, and the subtle difference of the cultural content expressed in the languages. Thus, translation cannot but encounter the problem of culture and its representation. In speaking of literary translation, a literary work which is not so popular in its source language could become extremely popular in the target language largely due to the effort made by its translator in representing not only its original meaning but also its cultural connotation and the cultural soil on which the work is received. We all know that Chinese culture, especially its representative classical literature, is characterized by a subtle richness full of artistic images, so its aesthetic spirit can only be perceived but not conveyed in another language that does not belong to the Chinese cultural tradition. Once it is conveyed in another language, not only will its original beauty be lost, but it will produce some new significance out of the misrepresentation, which finds particular embodiment in the English translation of such classical Chinese literary works as *Honglou meng* (A Dream of Red Mansions) and *Taohua yuan ji* (The Peach Blossom Spring).

To observe translation in the context of cultural studies might therefore well lead to the expansion of the domain of traditional translation studies, which has been rather limited to many of the Chinese translators and translation scholars. That is, it will expand from the original literal translation to the current cultural translation, and from passive conveyance to dynamic interpretation and even theoretical construction. But how should we reconstruct the definition of translation studies from the disciplinary perspective? Here, I would venture to offer my humble opinion on this issue from a new perspective. In view of the long-standing marginality of translation, its study is actually a *marginal* discipline between social science, natural science and the humanities: In the sense of its positivistic quantitative analysis and micro-perspective observation, it is undoubtedly a sub-discipline belonging to *social science*; in the sense of its relations with the mass media and its function in the age of globalization and high technology and computer science, it cannot avoid being affected by *natural science*; and in the sense of its broad connotation of cultural translation and interpretive function, it is obviously related to the *humanities*. Such an interdisciplinary feature and marginal characteristics certainly give rise to the indeterminacy of the concept of translation studies, which is both advantageous and disadvantageous: Anyone engaged in foreign language teaching or research could regard himself or herself as a translation scholar when he or she cannot be included in a specific discipline; similarly, translation scholars could do research in their respective disciplines or from theoretical perspectives. This is the paradox and tension in the definition of translation studies, on the grounds of which we could further our consideration and redefinition of this branch of learning from the perspective of cultural studies.

CULTURAL RELATIVISM RECONSTRUCTED IN REGARD TO TRANSLATION STUDIES

Since translation studies is first of all concerned with culture, we should recognize the relativity of culture, or cultural relativism, in its new global sense. As is well-known, cultural relativism has recently aroused the interest and theoretical debate in international academic circles once again, but this old issue has been endowed with new significance in the context of current cultural studies, stepping out of the narrow Eurocentric or West-centric domain into a much broader cross-cultural sphere. Although cultural studies is not a well-defined discipline, nor is it of a definite body of theory, it has been developing recently by leaps and bounds in North American academic circles. It is characterized by its interdisciplinariness which is certainly appropriate enough to include translation studies. Its reaction to cultural relativism lies in that it enables us to reach such a conclusion through observing the broad periphery outside of the centre: Every culture exists in relation to another culture; every culture has its own strengths and weaknesses; and no culture can avoid undergoing such stages as those of germination, development, prime and decline. So no one culture can dominate world culture. Similarly, there is no such thing as the one-dimensional influence of one culture on, or penetration into, another culture. As Oriental culture and Occidental culture usually influence each other, when one of these is in the state of temporary forcefulness, it might well influence the other, but even so, such influence is mutual and largely depends on the other's dynamic and creative reception. According to Edward Said, the "Orient was almost a European invention, and had been since antiquity a place of romance, exotic beings, haunting memories and landscapes, remarkable experiences".[6] In this sense, Orientalism is actually a "constructed" concept, which "stands forth and away from the Orient: that Orientalism makes sense at all depends more on the West than on the Orient, and this sense is directly indebted to various Western techniques of representation that made the Orient visible, clear, 'there' in discourse about it".[7] But the existence of this image or cultural construction has, to a certain extent, helped Western people to confront the objective existence of this phenomenon. Along with the deeper understanding of the Orient by Western people, the falsehood of Orientalism has become more and more conspicuous. This is the very significance that cultural relativism, after the 30-year debate on postmodernism and then postcolonialism on the international scale, has produced, which might well enlighten us in our translation studies in a cross-cultural context.

In the field of translation studies, scholars' understanding of translation in its traditional sense has been undergoing a shift of sorts, from focusing on literal translation to focusing on cultural translation, which will become dominant in the circles of China's translation studies. Therefore, the research on translation actually involves culture, especially concerning comparative studies between two cultures. I believe that the rise and fall of translation studies in recent years is closely related to the position of cultural studies and the role it plays in academic circles. When the "Eurocentric" mode of thinking dominates our research, we place particular emphasis on translating foreign culture for China, and our methodology always follows Western ways of academic research. We even try to communicate in a one-dimensional way with Western academia at the expense of our national cultural identity, which is by no means equitable communication with our Western colleagues. In the contemporary era, Western culture has shown signs of its inevitable crisis, and some far-sighted Western scholars have come to increasingly realize the aesthetic value and profound connotation of Oriental culture. Thus, it is the responsibility of translators to highlight the spirit and identity of Oriental culture, enabling it to engage in equitable dialogue with Western culture. In this sense, the rise of Oriental culture does not necessarily mean writing off Western culture, but rather co-existing with the latter on the same level, and communicating and having equitable dialogue with Western culture. At present, from the Chinese perspective, our emphasis should be particularly on introducing Chinese culture and literature abroad, so as to let more people know about China and Chinese culture in a truthful way. Only in this way can we promote mutual understanding with our Western colleagues. And in view of this, translation is an indispensable means for us to deal with comparative studies between different cultures and literatures, especially between Oriental and Occidental cultures. Cultural studies is thus the very ground on which different cultures, different disciplines and branches of learning and different fields of art and representation can carry out dialogues. The postmodernism debate in China and other Oriental or Third World countries in recent years has undoubtedly broken through the "Eurocentric" or "West-centric" mode of thinking, paving the way for us to question Western postmodern theory with Third World writing experience and cultural phenomena, while the discussion and research on the issue of postcolonialism or postcoloniality accelerate the process of decolonizing Oriental and Third World culture.[8] Since cultural studies points to contemporary non-elite culture, it will help us to question the traditional "Eurocentric" canon formation, moving Oriental culture from the periphery to the centre and deconstructing the myth of the so-called monolithic centre. Hence, it is of vital significance to translate Oriental culture for the whole world.

Let us take into consideration current Chinese cultural and intellectual life in regard to our translation studies. For the past ten years or more, remarkable achievements have been made in China's cultural and literary studies, which proves that it is a historical tendency to have theoretical dialogues between East and West. Therefore, the rise of cultural studies has not only crossed the boundaries between literature and culture, between language and representation, and between Eastern culture and Western culture, but has also deconstructed

24

the artificial gap between the periphery and the centre, making it favourable for Oriental culture and literature to move from the periphery to the centre of the world. From a disciplinary point of view, translation studies in China has long been associated with either linguistics or literary studies, and it is not even recognized in some universities.[9] Comparative literature, which flourished in China in the early 1980s, helped to legitimize translation studies as media studies. The current prevalence of cultural studies has more or less obscured the boundary between linguistics and literary studies, paving the way for a new discipline—translatology—to rise in China's academic circles. Taking this into account, what do we think of the state of the art of translation studies in China? It is obviously far from satisfactory. Some translators would rather spend much time "re-translating" the canonical literary works at the expense of letting some excellent newly published contemporary literary works go untranslated. Translators would rather do repeated translations of foreign language works into Chinese than vice versa, with the latter being more difficult and involving more time and energy. Quite a few translation scholars are still interested in endless debates on the shallow technical level in translation practice or the subjective evaluation of the Chinese versions of foreign literary works. Such debates can never reach an adequate conclusion, for they seem to neglect a common fact; that is, truth can only be approached rather than finalized. Countless relative truths amount to the absolute truth. Meanwhile, such endless debates are far from reaching a theoretical and academic peak. There is much to do in translation studies from a cross-cultural point of view. In this sense, cultural studies can at least provide us with a new perspective from which we can push forward translation studies in China, enabling us to move to a higher level and transcend the "either/or" mode of thinking in an attempt to reach the conclusion that can be applied to explain all the cultural phenomena in the East and West. Only by putting translation studies in the broad context of cultural studies can it approach the level of enabling equitable dialogue with the international translation scholarship.

TRANSLATION AND THE DEMARGINALIZATION OF CHINESE CULTURE

It is true that cultural studies is characterized by the deconstruction of artificial binary opposition, such as the opposition between elite culture and popular culture, enabling the intellectuals shouldering the task of enlightenment to step out of the isolated intellectual ivory tower and involve themselves in the broad masses of people. In this way, they will first identify themselves as one of the people and then realize their ideal of "post-enlightenment". It also crosses the border between Oriental culture and Occidental culture, making it possible for them to communicate and have dialogues. Translation is no doubt an indispensable means to realize this aim. But unfortunately, there has been an imbalance in China's cultural and literary translation, with many more translations of foreign culture than of Chinese culture, the simple reason being the fact that Chinese people know much more about the West than Western people know about China. But even so, Occidentalism has become a mysterious concept or phenomenon among quite a number of Chinese people, especially those young people who do not have much knowledge about the West and its culture.[10] As far as translation itself is concerned, we have more skilled translators introducing Western culture into China than vice versa. Particularly in recent years, affected by contemporary commercializing trends, many of the young translators do not spend much time laying a solid foundation in foreign languages, so they have difficulty translating Chinese culture into Western languages. To my mind, judging whether one's command of foreign languages is good or poor only takes into account whether he or she can translate Chinese works into foreign languages well, or whether he or she can directly communicate with the international scholarship in idiomatic foreign languages. If this can be done, I think it may be the most significant contribution a translator can make to the construction of Chinese culture.

Last but not least, I will say a few words about the so-called "decolonization" of Chinese culture, about which there have been heated debates among domestic and overseas scholars in translation studies and comparative literature studies. Here, I still maintain my stand: Chinese culture, which is profound in content and splendid and rich in heritage, cannot be "colonized" although it has been largely "Europeanized" or "Westernized" since the beginning of this century.[11] It is true that we lack our own critical discourse and have borrowed a lot of our cultural and literary criticism according to some scholars. Also, it is true that we have to publish our research results in the international language—English—which is said to have "colonized" the Chinese language and Chinese culture largely due to the advent of globalization and the popularity of the Internet. But it is an inevitable stage through which Chinese culture must pass to become more mature and to approach the mainstream of world culture. So it is unnecessary to launch a campaign to "decolonize" Chinese culture and its language, which may well give rise to a new state of isolating China from the international community. We should not, however, neglect another fact: In world culture, the Chinese culture is still in an inadequate position of marginality whose value has by no means been fully recognized by the world, with the exception of a few sinologists who usually have a deep understanding of certain aspects of Chinese culture but lack a comprehensive grasp of the Chinese cultural and aesthetic spirit. Therefore, it may help Chinese culture to move from the periphery to the centre and deconstruct the myth of the monolithic centre if we begin to "demarginalize" and "deterritorialize" Chinese culture by starting with translation and its studies. If this can be done in an adequate manner, it would put Chinese culture in a favourable position of engaging in equitable dialogues with Western culture as well as with the international scholarship. Hence, the function of translation and its studies in our era of globalization can never be replaced by any other branches of learning or any other means of communication.

Globalizing Chinese Literature: Toward a Rewriting of Contemporary Chinese Literary Culture

In recent years, after the theoretical debate on the question of postmodernism and postmodernity in the Chinese context, discussing the issue of modernity in both the West and China has become another theoretical topic for us Chinese literary scholars and intellectuals, especially in regard to the issue of postmodernism or postmodernity of Chinese characteristics. We are now in a new century, as well as a new millennium. What is characteristic of our age? Obviously, different scholars, from their own perspectives, have described it in different ways. In my view, it is certainly appropriate to call the present time an age of globalization, which has already manifested itself in many fields, even in our field of literary and cultural studies in the Chinese context.[1] In such an age, intellectuals, writers, critics and literary and cultural studies scholars cannot but take pains to conceive or picture the future orientation of culture and its elite form—literature—since elite literature is being challenged by popular literature and culture, and literary studies by cultural studies. As a Chinese scholar dealing both with comparative literature and cultural studies, what I am most concerned about is the new orientation of Chinese literature studies, or more specifically, contemporary Chinese literature studies, as this sub-branch of Chinese studies is more closely related to the age of globalization, in which we can first observe modern Chinese literature in the broad context of world literature and achieve a rewriting of contemporary Chinese literary culture from an international and comparative point of view. Of course, when I mention literature or literary studies in general, I simply refer to elite or canonical literature and its studies.

CONTEMPORARY LITERATURE CHALLENGED BY POPULAR CULTURE

In current Chinese cultural and intellectual circles, talking a lot about globalization has become a fashion. But in the present chapter, I am limiting it to the field of literary and cultural studies as it has certainly exerted a strong influence in this field. Thus, globalization could be viewed as an academic and theoretical discourse in the contemporary era and a reaction to the discourse of modernity and postmodernity if we just focus on globalization and its effect on literature and culture. It is first of all a process of capitalization in which the national economy is either engulfed by global capitalization or has lost its competitiveness. The same is true of cultural and literary production under the impact of globalization. In the age of globalization, those less influential cultures are losing their national identity under the impact of globalization, and serious literature is confronted by various challenges which even threaten the survival of literature as a canonical product of elite culture. Literature and literary studies are in an unprecedented unfavourable situation. This cannot but remind me of the literary and cultural situation at the turn of the twentieth century. In speaking of literature at the turn of the new century, we cannot but think of the term *fin de siècle*, for literature of the *fin de siècle* always reminds us of the decadent literary trends in the previous turn of the century. It sometimes even discourages people who love literature and who are very much worried about whether literature will come to an end in the future. It is therefore not surprising for people to raise such a question: Will literature, in its elite sense, in the new century or in the new millennium be what it used to be at the turn of the last century? If not, then what will the future orientation of literature and literary studies be as it is now severely challenged by popular culture and cultural studies which largely points to popular and consumer culture? As for this, I will first of all reflect on the status quo of the contemporary Chinese literary situation at the threshold of the new century, where I will deal with elite literary studies and its interaction with cultural studies. Then I will go back to modern Chinese literature, which we will explore in the broad context of world literature.

In the past few years, especially since the international postmodernism debate swept China in the latter part of the 1980s, the rise of popular culture has upset more and more scholars of canonical literature in current China. Of course, the marketization and commercialization are also responsible for the prevalence of popular culture and literature in contemporary China. We can easily find a remarkable phenomenon in Chinese cultural and intellectual life, especially after China's involvement in the socialist market economy at the beginning of the 1990s. Postmodernism of "Chinese characteristics" has been transformed from the once-dominant *avant-garde* intellectual rebelling against traditional realist and modernist literary conventions to the challenge raised by popular culture against elite culture and literature. The increasingly shrinking literary market is filled with various books of *"petites histoires"*[2] rather than those of "master narrative". And in the face of cultural globalization, serious literary writing is being challenged by the so-called "Internet literature" and consumer culture. Serious writers can hardly find an environment similar to that in the New Period (*Xin shiqi*) when writing for life's sake or for art's sake dominated writers' creative consciousness. To this, Chinese men of letters and literary scholars respond or react in different ways and even argue among themselves because many of them are not fully prepared for such a sudden change in their work and lives. Some of them simply view this change as a sort of negative escape from political and social responsibility, which is characterized by the undermining of Chinese modernity since the May 4th period in 1919 which marked the beginning of the new Chinese culture and literature. They are obviously not satisfied with the drastic change in Chinese literary tradition caused by the May 4th Movement. So what they want to do is to reverse the historical verdict of that significant cultural and literary movement. But that is apparently impossible, for it was in the May 4th period that Chinese literature started its movement toward the world stage and gradually became part of world literature. Chinese literature began to step out of its isolated state and faced the impact from various foreign, especially Western, literary currents and cultural and academic trends. So it is not strange that other more open-minded scholars take a different attitude toward the rise of popular culture and literature, looking upon it as a remarkable beginning for intellectuals to seek a new public sphere in a long-territorialized political and cultural domain, and for writers to depend on their own creative products rather than upon the support, both political and financial, offered by the government. They enthusiastically welcome the arrival of this cultural plurality onto China's cultural and literary scene, for they will be able to write in a comparatively free cultural atmosphere, experimenting with various kinds of writing styles and narrative techniques, and exploring the comparatively old issue of rewriting the history of modern Chinese literature from new perspectives.

It is true that the so-called cultural globalization manifests itself more and more clearly, which is closely related to the sweeping of postmodernism worldwide, especially in the form of popular culture. As we know, postmodernism usually points to these two poles: the *avant-garde* intellectual rebelling against the established order and convention, and the popular and consumer culture challenging elite culture and literature. These two trends were once juxtaposed in a parallel way in the West. But the Chinese case is somewhat different from what has happened in the Western context. As a matter of fact, the rise of popular culture and literature in China is nothing but a historical trend beyond one's expectation and resistance in such a transitional period of cultural transformation, in which the dominant literary code has changed from the code of the New Period to that of the Post-New Period (*Hou xin shiqi*): The former is known for writing for art's and life's sake and the latter known for writing for the sake of readers and the market. It is also marked by various symbols of post-industrial society although China is still largely far from being postmodern despite its modernization progress in many areas. Even so, we are still confronted with such a pluralistically oriented literary situation: The *avant-garde* experimentation with narrative devices and writing technique is still going on, although in a more limited sphere; the new realist fiction appeals to the taste of contemporary readers who prefer the real life proper rather than a selected and typified form of the realities; popular literature is expanding its market but its value of the aesthetic cannot last for long; and film production and the TV industry and other forms of mass media pose severe challenges to canonical literature and culture on the one hand, but on the other hand, they are actually helping to popularize canonical literature in one way or another so that it can attract a greater audience in the future. So we can say that the more advances made in science and technology, the more people desire the enjoyment of the aesthetic, especially from literary works. Actually, literature can never come to an end, even in the present age of globalization when literature and elite literary studies are suffering

31

from the ruthless "law of jungle" as long as there are people to write and read literary works.

In the face of the above-mentioned phenomenon that is unfavourable for the development of elite literature, literary scholars and critics are, on the one hand, naturally very much worried about the future of literature and, on the other hand, trying to think of some strategies to lift literary creation in the contemporary era out of its present crisis. In my opinion, the current cultural and literary situation characterized by elite literature being challenged by popular culture is such a case, not only in China but also in other parts of the world. As for the question of whether literature, in its canonical sense, could still survive in the face of the challenge from popular culture, my answer is always optimistic, even in the present situation which is unfavourable to elite literature. I believe that literature will still exist and never be degraded as long as there are people to read and enjoy it, for what is expressed in literary representation cannot be replaced by other means of art although the domain of elite literary creation is becoming narrower and narrower.[3] Just as Harold Bloom, perhaps the last defender of canonical literature at the moment, has insightfully pointed out, "All literary tradition has been necessarily elitist, in every period, if not because the Scene of Instruction always depends upon a primal choosing and a being chosen which is what 'elite' means." The survival of literature is just like the relationship between teacher and student: "No teacher, however impartial he or she attempts to be, can avoid choosing among students, or being chosen by them, for this is the very nature of teaching. Literary teaching is precisely like literature itself; no strong writer can choose his precursors until first he is chosen by them, and no strong student can fail to be chosen by his teacher."[4] It is true that elite culture and its product literature are being severely challenged by popular culture and literature, but I always hold that popular and fashionable things cannot always be popular. When the trend is out of fashion, those really valuable products will certainly remain in the history of culture and literature, while those of superficial value will sooner or later be erased from the memory of the new generation of readers. Chinese literature in the new millennium will still exist although it will certainly take on a different look: It will not appear as the instrument of enlightenment for only a few intellectual elites as it used to be, but rather a means of aesthetic enjoyment for the broader audience; and it will not be so powerful as to push forward social change and promote economic reform, but rather function in its limited—but not so narrow—

sphere, with its beauty and aesthetic taste appealing to certain people. Since literary creation is like this, the function of literary studies should not be inadequately exaggerated at all, and literary history should only be written as the history of literature rather than as that of ideology or political movement. In this sense, I think it is necessary to re-examine modern and contemporary Chinese literature in the broad context of global culture or world literature as it has always been argued about by both domestic and overseas scholars.

A NEW PERIODIZATION OF MODERN CHINESE LITERATURE

Having realized the importance and irreplaceability of literature as well as literary studies, I think it is now necessary to first re-examine modern Chinese literature from a new theoretical perspective as it has always been under the Western influence since the beginning of the twentieth century, or more exactly, after the May 4th Movement when a new Chinese literature started in a completely different direction, moving gradually toward the world stage. In this section, inspired by the aesthetics of reception and the New Historicist doctrine, I try to re-describe twentieth-century Chinese literature which, to my mind, should be observed within the framework of global culture or world literature. For in my view, the traditional writing of modern and contemporary Chinese literary history has a fatal shortcoming; that is, those politically oriented literary historians always identify literary history with political or ideological history, thus ignoring the internal logic and law of development of literature and culture proper. I will continue to deal with this problem later on when I discuss the re-periodization of contemporary Chinese literature in the next section. Unlike many of my Chinese colleagues, my strategy is to view twentieth-century Chinese literature as a code of the time and culture, which, in the broad context of world literature, is actually a process of moving toward the world stage and trying to identify with world literature in the process of cultural globalization.

As is well-known, Chinese literature has a long history and splendid cultural and aesthetic heritage. But along with the swift development of the West after the Renaissance period, Chinese culture and literature became, for a long time, "marginalized". Upon entering the twentieth century, Chinese literary scholars became more and more aware of this "marginalized" position that Chinese literature had in the broad context of world literature. In order to recapture its lost grandeur, it should move from the periphery to the centre by identifying with the then popular Western cultural modernity or modern Western literature. That is why they largely called for the translation of Western literary works and cultural and academic thoughts, viewing this practice as the best way of getting China out of its isolated state. A famous slogan was the so-called "grabbism" (*nalai zhuyi*); that is, "grabbing" anything useful to us. By means of such large-scale translation, all the major cultural trends or literary currents—romanticism, realism and modernism—which dominated Western literary circles for over a hundred years, as well as their representative works of art and their authors, were introduced to China, exerting a profound influence on twentieth-century Chinese literature at the threshold of cultural modernity.[5] Undoubtedly, such an effort to translate Western literature did promote the process of internationalization or globalization[6] of modern Chinese literature, giving Chinese literature of this period a different look from its traditional counterpart. Unfortunately, this sort of modernization, internationalization or globalization is only individually oriented, without reaching the level of mutual communication and equitable dialogue. As we all know, due to the fact that in the broad context of world literature, it is the Western discourse that has dominated the orientation of world literature, the movement of Chinese literature toward the world stage is actually one of Westernization, just like the eastward globalization of economy and culture. But in this process, national culture alternates between strong and weak, forming an interaction with globalization, or what we could call "glocalization". Without realizing this objective phenomenon and by just over-emphasizing the action of any one aspect while overlooking the other's reaction, we cannot grasp the orientation of contemporary world culture and literature in a precise way, let alone periodize modern Chinese literature in a relevant way.

Now that we have realized the distinction of the international background of modern Chinese literature, I will put forward my own re-periodization of the Chinese literature of this era. I still hold that modern Chinese literature originated in the May 4th Movement in 1919, not only because of the significance of the political event, but because this was the most open period in the history of twentieth-century Chinese literature as well as cultural and intellectual life. It was in this very period that Chinese literature started to have a consciousness of totality and internationalization. That is, many Chinese scholars or literary critics opine that Chinese literature of this period is no longer an isolated phenomenon, but part of world literature. Any periodization or re-periodization of Chinese literature of the time cannot avoid its unseparated connections with the May 4th Movement. As far as the positive and negative significance of this movement is concerned, literary historians and scholars still have different opinions. According to the summary of some overseas scholars, liberal intellectuals think of it as a movement of literary renaissance, religious reform and enlightenment, while conservative nationalists and traditionalists regard it as a disaster of the Chinese nation; to the Chinese Communist Party, the May 4th Movement is always viewed as an anti-Imperialist and anti-feudalist movement.[7] But just as Wang Yuanhua points out, "The 'May 4th' contains two aspects: one points to the students' movement that took place in Beijing in 1919, and the other to the ideological movement started in 1916. The former is usually called the 'May 4th' National Salvation Movement, and the latter 'May 4th' New Cultural Movement."[8] That is, the former—the May 4th Movement—should be viewed as a historical incident characterized by anti-Imperialism and anti-feudalism, and the latter—the May 4th Cultural Movement—should be regarded as a cultural and literary movement characterized by the revolution and Westernization of culture. Here, Wang obviously intends to highlight the cultural and literary significance of the May 4th Movement. Obviously, Wang's distinction is opposed by quite a few overseas scholars, chiefly because he is said to have neglected the very part played by the May 4th Movement in the history of modern Chinese thinking.[9] If we just consider the significance of the May 4th Movement from the historical perspective of modern Chinese thinking, this criticism seems reasonable. But if we want to replace the periodization of literary history with that of ideological history or the history of thought, then it will run counter to the internal logic of literary development. According to what Wang originally means, two aspects of the May 4th Movement are emphasized at the same time: the significance of enlightenment in the history of thought and that of periodization of cultural and literary history, with modernity as the intermediary between the two. Thus, the May 4th Movement also marked the beginning of China's modernity, indicating that China had been involved in the process of comprehensive internationality and modernity in politics, economy, society and culture. This undoubtedly gave rise to China's enthusiastic involvement in the process of (economic) globalization in the late twentieth century. This is also probably the very reason why some conservative intellectuals always accuse the May 4th Movement of starting a sort of cultural colonization and "overall Westernization" (*quanpan xihua*). Nevertheless, the important part played by the May 4th Movement in promoting China's cultural modernity process has been eloquently proved by history.

It is true that only around the May 4th period did such an "overall Westernization" reach its peak although Lin Shu, Liang Qichao, Lu Xun and Hu Shi had already advocated the translation of as much Western literature and cultural and theoretical trends as possible before that time. Talking a lot about Schopenhauer, Bergson, Nietzsche and Freud was an academic fashion among intellectuals and even quite a number of writers and critics. So today's comparatists and scholars of translation studies might well view the translated literature at the time as an inseparable part of modern Chinese literature, for as far as the source of its wide influence is concerned, many modern Chinese writers were more influenced or inspired by foreign writers rather than by domestic literary tradition. The novel writing technique and various new devices utilized by the Western modernists and *avant-garde* permeated the Chinese writers' creative consciousness and sub-consciousness and thus became part of Chinese writing technique and creative practice. Take Lu Xun, for example, who describes the beginning of his writing career in a figurative way:

> But when I began to write novels, I did not realize that I [had] the talent [for] writing fiction. For at the time, I stayed in the guest house in Beijing, where I could not write research papers as I did not have any references, nor could I do translation as I did not even have the original texts at hand. In this way, what I could do [was] to write something like fiction. Hence *The Diary of the Mad Man* came out. When I wrote this piece, I only depended on some hundred foreign literary works I had read and some knowledge of medicine I had obtained. As for other preparations, just no more.[10]

The same is true of many other Chinese writers of the May 4th period. They would rather admit that they were influenced by Western literature than by traditional Chinese literature. We could say that Lu Xun's words are frank enough as to represent at least quite a few writers of the May 4th period. This is also one of the important reasons why some conservative scholars severely criticize the May 4th Movement for starting a sort of cultural "colonization" and linguistic "Europeanization". But historically speaking, any newly born idea or artistic innovation would at first experience a long period of illegitimacy, but along with the elapse of time and examination of practice as well as its own effort to legitimize itself, this illegitimate concept would become legitimate, thereby moving from the periphery to the centre. Today's scholars of modern Chinese literature, no matter what attitude they might have toward the May 4th Movement, will probably not suspect that it was the beginning of modern Chinese literature. As for the end of this period, I think it should be marked by the end of the Cultural Revolution in 1976 rather than the founding of the People's Republic of China in 1949, not only because of the fact that it is reasonable to assume that contemporary literature started over 20 years ago—thus coinciding with the logic of literary periodization—but more because of the broad context of world literature of which Chinese literature should be regarded as a part.

After 1976, there appeared the second wave of "openness" and "moving toward the world" in Chinese literature, or the so-called second "overall Westernization" as is described by some overseas scholars. We can simply see the difference between the beginning of the first "overall Westernization" in 1919 and that of the second one after 1976: The former is characterized by a sort of modernity, and the latter a sort of postmodernity if we do not want to separate the latter totally from the former. That is, despite the huge difference between the modern and postmodern even in the Western context, the postmodern should be observed within the broad context of the modern, for it still has close connections with the latter. In China, this characteristic is even more apparent: Contemporary Chinese literature written after 1976 is called New Period literature, or literature of the New Era, with different cultural codes in co-existence rather than only one being dominant.[11] As a result, contemporary Chinese literature is positioned closer to the mainstream of world literature, moving toward the world stage in a more conscious way, in the process of which it is carrying out dialogues with literatures of all countries, especially that of Western countries, and trying to be an important part of world literature. Internationally, especially in the world of Western literature and culture, the postmodernism debate which started in the late 1950s and early 1960s was at the time undergoing a shift from North American cultural and literary circles to European ideological and philosophical circles.[12] Those involved in the debate were, either clearly or vaguely, aware that literary modernism, which had been on the decline immediately after World War II, had gradually come to an end. As a new *episteme* or cultural dominant, postmodernism had completely taken the dominant place of modernism. Similarly, cultural modernity as a project of enlightenment was also in a profound crisis, which was first questioned and challenged by the rising of postmodernity in the post-industrial society, and then lashed by the wave of globalization in the late 1980s. As a historical discourse, globalization has obviously taken the place of the discourse of modernity and postmodernity. So in such a broad context, that Chinese literature has entered the contemporary period completely coincides with the internal logic of its development. This is also in agreement with its specific international background. This has eloquently proved that Chinese literature is no longer isolated, but rather involved in the mainstream of world literature and manifests itself with its unique grandeur and appeal in the forest of world literature. A comparative history of world literature cannot but include the achievements made in Chinese literary creation and theory and criticism, otherwise it will not be regarded as being objective or comprehensive. The advent of globalization has not only provided Chinese intellectuals with precious opportunities to communicate more easily with the outside world, but also enabled us literary scholars and historians to rethink twentieth-century Chinese literature, viewing it as part of an immediate past which cannot influence our way of thinking and writing in the present time.

RE-PERIODIZING CONTEMPORARY CHINESE LITERATURE

From the above description and discussion, we can see that the so-called New Period literature is nothing but another name for contemporary Chinese literature. Now I would like to elaborate my re-periodization of contemporary Chinese literature written since 1976, which is somewhat different from that of many of my Chinese colleagues. To my mind, Chinese literature written since the end of the Cultural Revolution can be further categorized into these phases: (1) the Pre-New Period (*qian xinshiqi*, 1976–1978), during which the main code and discourse were still close to those of the Cultural Revolution, and which served as a transitional stage; (2) the High New Period (*sheng xinshiqi*, 1979–1989), which was the most prosperous time for Chinese literature of the twentieth century during which the main code or spirit was that of enlightenment and modernity in its Chinese sense, and literature and culture were developing in a comparatively pluralistic orientation; (3) the Post-New Period (1990 to present), which obviously runs counter to the main *Zeitgeist* of the High New Period and during which the cultural dominant has been changing from modern to postmodern, with literary writing becoming more and more pragmatic and market-oriented. Now, along with the impact of globalization on the Chinese economy as well as intellectual and cultural life, literary culture is becoming increasingly different from that of the New Period.

The first phase, from 1976 to 1978, was the so-called Pre-New Period, which was the phase when Chinese literature had just set foot in the New Period, and during which literature was still strongly coloured with the dominant of the Cultural Revolution. Even the criterion for the evaluation of literary works and the critical discourse followed on from the ten-year Cultural Revolution, with the exception of some "underground" literary texts. It is true that the New Period at this phase itself was a reaction to the old leftist literary doctrine, but there were still elements of both continuity and discontinuity from the previous period. From an international point of view, Chinese literature at this stage started with the revival of realism in its traditional sense. The main task for literary theorists and critics is to critically inherit excellent literary classics, both domestic and foreign, and re-establish the realistic aesthetic principle as the only criterion for evaluating literary works. If a literary work is written under the guidance of this principle, it is evaluated as an "excellent" and "healthy" work of art, otherwise it is labelled as being "sick" or "misleading". In literary creation, greater emphasis is laid chiefly on the deepening of the ideological content rather than the experimentation with new writing techniques and artistic devices running counter to the realistic aesthetic. Even so, artistic exploration in new writing techniques and devices are emphasized in the literary field as quite a few writers already pay considerable attention to the employment of the stream-of-consciousness technique and psychological monologues in their writing. Judging by this, we could say that this was a transitional or even preparatory phase for Chinese literature to usher in a completely new era.

The second phase, from 1979 to 1989, was the so-called High New Period. Along with the debate on the criterion of examining the truth and then the Third Plenary Session of the 11th CPC Central Committee, the artificial forbidden areas of research were dissolved, and tremendous changes took place in both literary content and aesthetic form which were viewed as a reflection of official ideology. Internationally, faced with foreign influences, especially the Western influence as a direct consequence of the introduction and translation of Western trends of literature and culture, writers and critics became very conscious of their social responsibility to describe social reality and create artistic innovation. Although literature of this phase was still marked with political colour and even restricted to political power and ideology, it established its authority as a relatively autonomous entity independent of any other factors. Referring to the internal logic of the evolution of world literature, we can see clearly that the cultural dominant of Chinese literature of this phase was obviously characterized by modernity; that is, literature had already stepped out of the one-dimensional emphasis on deepening the literary content and ideological connotation and appealed to the exploration of, and experimentation with, artistic devices and writing technique. This finds particular embodiment in the rise of a group of *avant-garde* novelists and poets, especially in their literary ideas and manifestos. As a matter of fact, with these two forces entering the world of literary creation and criticism, literature was marked by the rise of modernity and its immediate decline after reaching its prime. In theory and criticism, discussions or debates on such issues as the new aesthetic principles[13] and humanism and alienation more or less touched upon some problems beyond the dominant of the New Period. The latter part of this phase, I would say, was obviously marked by the dominant of the Post-New Period. But in any event, as a summary of the literature of a certain phase, the High New Period is one of the rare periods in the history of twentieth-century Chinese literature in which remarkable achievements were made. Chinese literature was moving toward the world stage with a sense of increasing globality; literary theory and criticism also caught up with its development in the Western context, with the appearance of the so-called New Historical–Aesthetic Criticism (*xin lishi meixue piping*), New Tide Criticism (*xinchao piping*) and Academic Criticism (*xueyuan piping*).[14] Theoretical dialogues between Chinese and Western scholars were made possible to a large extent. It should be admitted that the cultural dominant of the High New Period was the humanistic spirit or humanism, with literature enjoying its independent position despite the external interference. Along with the rise of *avant-garde* fiction, however, such humanism was obviously challenged, with rebellious voices different from the cultural dominant being heard now and then in the field of literature and art, and different narrative discourses and cultural codes being read in quite a few literary texts. Moreover, with the impact of various factors outside of literature proper—political, economic and even cultural—the permeation of high technology in an intellectual atmosphere of the cyberspace and the strong influence of Western postmodernist cultural trends all paved the way for the changing of the dominant from the New Period to the Post-New Period. Toward the latter part of the 1980s, with the gradual decline of the postmodernism debate in Western cultural and literary circles, postmodernism apparently lost its appeal, and all the subaltern discourses, including postcolonial and diasporic discourses and lesbian studies, repressed in the very "periphery", were moving to the "centre" in an attempt to decentralize the Imperial hegemonic discourse. People might well still regard these trends as being closely related to postmodernism in its broad sense. Undoubtedly, this was an age of international cultural transformation characterized by different forces competing against one another and co-existing. The long-ignored cultural relativism and cultural pluralism once again dominated the cultural scene in the "Post-Cold War" period. Affected by all the above elements, contemporary Chinese literature changed from being the dominant of the New Period to that of the Post-New Period.

Then came the third phase, which started in 1990—the so-called Post-New Period—about which quite a number of Chinese critics and scholars still have doubts despite the fact that some of them have also tried to periodize contemporary Chinese literature from their own theoretical perspectives.[15] What they want to point out is that the New Period cannot go on indefinitely. In view of this or some other strategies of discourse, they have to provide another term to describe this intermediary period between the New Period and another era largely different from the previous one in cultural and aesthetic code. As I am involved in this literary periodization and the theoretical debate about it, I have to offer my own concept. What I would like to point out here, however, is that, unlike the New Period which is deeply marked by political colour, the Post-New Period is first of all a cultural concept rather than a political one, which is used to exclusively deal with the periodization of contemporary Chinese literature. So it should not be restricted to the power of mainstream ideology or any other authoritative discourse. It is created by the autonomous law of literary evolution in a given cultural atmosphere. That is to say, putting forward the concept of the Post-New Period is preconditioned theoretically by the development of literature and culture rather than anything else. Understanding this concept, therefore, should point to these different levels: the natural continuity in time and discontinuity in literary code, with the latter being more conspicuous. More precisely, from the chronological perspective, the Post-New Period comes after the end of the High New Period, while from the perspective of the law of literary development and the changing of the cultural dominant, it goes against the direction of the former or, to some extent, poses a sort of challenge to the cultural dominant of the New Period. Such a challenge against, and discontinuity with, the New Period finds particular embodiment in the following aspects:

(1)   The radical experimentation made by the *avant-garde* writing forms a severe challenge against the humanistic spirit of the New Period, with the self-identity of "Man" being lost and literature becoming more and more formalistic technique-oriented, which is aimed at deconstructing the depth structure of New Period literature. Many of the texts not only run counter to the traditional aesthetic principle but mock and parody the modernist aesthetic principle, and some even fall into the impasse of anti-interpretation, anti-form and anti-art, which finds particular embodiment in the poetic form made by those "avant-gardist" or "trans-avant-gardist" poets appearing after the fall of the "Misty Poetry" (*menglong shi*). In their texts, the anti-functionalist attempt has been pushed to the very extreme.

(2)   The rise of the New Realist Fiction and its continuous development are in effect not only a strong reaction to the radical experimentation made by the avant-gardists, but a sort of transcendence over the traditional realistic aesthetic principle. This should also be regarded as highlighting a "sense of commonality" during the turn of the century and reaching a compromise with the reading public. But on the other hand, the rise of the New Realist Fiction has realized the aesthetic ideal characterized by narrowing the gap between elite literature and popular literature, which is similar to the attempt at "crossing the border and closing the gap" made by the early American postmodernists like Leslie Fiedler.

(3)   The impact made by the contemporary commercializing trend is aimed at filling the natural gap between elite literature and popular literature, but it has created another dilemma for current literary

42

creation: no compromise with the commercialization at the expense of literary creation, and no catering to the new cultural-economic atmosphere at the expense of giving up the unique quality of elite literature. In this respect, popular literature devoted to the so-called "*petites histoires*"; media literature characterized by wide coverage of different aspects of life, including TV series and the film industry; and the entrusted literature characterized by historical narrative and advertisement, including reportage and journalism, have together formed a colourful picture in which different discourses co-exist and complement each other. In this sense, we could say that Chinese literature of the Post-New Period has really entered an age of pluralism and Bakhtinian "carnivalization" without the mainstream. That is, popular literature has more or less taken up some of the space occupied by serious literature in the 1990s. This phenomenon is developing in a parallel way with Western postmodernist literature although the latter is already on the decline after reaching its prime. It is both the summing up of a past age and the dawn of a new age. So this is only a transitional period which will come to an end once the transition is complete. It is undoubtedly a short period in which few great works of art will appear, but it will play an indispensable role in the history of contemporary Chinese literature whose value will be "discovered" by future researchers and historians of literature.

TOWARD A REWRITING OF CONTEMPORARY CHINESE LITERARY CULTURE

Although rewriting literary history is already an old topic both in the West as well as in China, to do it from a new global and theoretical perspective is still attractive to quite a few literary scholars. But in today's new age of globalization, reviewing this seemingly "old" issue from a new perspective is of certain relevance since tremendous changes have taken place in the past three decades. Undoubtedly, we are now in an age of globalization, both economically and culturally, with the latter aspect being more complicated. To many intellectuals, the future of literature and art is not so bright, nor could they survive in such an age of globalization. Even J. Hillis Miller, an eminent American literary scholar who is very interested in the destiny of literature and literary studies under the impact of globalization and telecommunications, expresses his pessimistic view about the future of literary studies. To him, "literary study's time is always up. It will survive as it has always survived, as a ghostly revenant, as a somewhat embarrassing or alarming spectral visitant at the feast of reason", but he then emphasizes more optimistically: "Nevertheless, though there's never time, though it's never the time, these holes, potholes or black holes, 'literature' as survivor, as a feature of absolute singularity within any cultural forms in whatever medium, will continue to demand urgently to be 'studied,' here and now, within whatever new institutional and departmental configurations we devise and within whatever new regime of telecommunications we inhabit."[16] In this way, we can see that as long as there are human beings who enjoy reading literature, literature has every reason to survive. The same is true of literary studies, but it will never create such a "cultural fever" as it did in the 1980s in China when the country just started to open itself up to the outside world and to practise economic reform.

As we all know, cultural globalization is apparently a direct consequence of economic globalization. It is characterized by the spreading of Western, especially American, culture all over the world. As a result, world culture is becoming more and more homogenized with weaker cultures' national identity gradually being lost. So it is not surprising that such a process is resisted by another force: cultural localization. As long as cultural globalization is in progress, it will be resisted by the efforts of cultural localization. World culture will develop in the context of these two forces being juxtaposed, conflicting and communicating alternately, but finally coming together to engage in dialogues and negotiations. In this way, we might well expect that in the context of globalization, the new framework of world culture in the twenty-first century will be characterized by different cultures engaging in dialogue and merging to some degree rather than the "cultural conflict" envisaged by Samuel Huntington in 1993.[17] Indeed, different cultures are developing in a pluralistic way although they could possibly be in harmonious co-existence. The same is true of literature and literary studies today. With this broad background, twentieth-century Chinese literature should be re-examined from an international and comparative perspective since we regard it as part of world literature. A new history of modern Chinese literature could thus be written in such an age. As for contemporary Chinese literature, which is still developing, we can only describe it but not write its history as it is too early for an evaluation.

Before concluding this chapter, I just want to say a few words about the significance of rewriting modern Chinese literary history and contemporary Chinese literary culture in the current age of globalization. Although the aesthetics of reception was on the decline in the late 1970s and early 1980s, it was immediately divided into three modes of literary study: writing of literary history centred on literary reception, the empirical study of literature based on the positivistic factor and experience, and reader-response criticism characterized by readers' affective response and dynamic interpretation. Among the three orientations, literary historiography undoubtedly occupies an important place, which has also influenced in a positive way the international collaborative project, *The Comparative History of Literature in European Languages*, under the auspices of the International Comparative Literature Association.[18] Rewriting literary history must be associated with issues of canon formation and reformation, or the fourth orientation of the future of literary theory, as was summed up by Ralph Cohen over ten years ago: "Seeking the New, Redefining the Old, and the Pleasures of Theory Writing."[19] That is to say, new interpretations from theoretical perspectives of canonical literary works should be offered, which is also a controversial issue debated among European and American scholars over the last ten years.[20] But what should be regarded as literary canon? How is the canon formed? What factors are behind the formation of the canon? We have to answer all these questions from theoretical perspectives before starting to rewrite contemporary Chinese literary culture. As for what should be regarded as the canon, Harold Bloom has insightfully pointed out that "the Canon, once we view it as the relation of an individual reader and writer to what has preserved out of what has been written, and forget the canon as a list of books for required study, will be seen as identical with the literary Art of Memory, not with the religious sense of canon".[21] Hence, the literary canon is composed of those excellent works of art produced by generation after generation of writers since ancient times. Those that are regarded as "canonical" works should be selected on the basis of three criteria: readers' reception and market success, recognition from critical circles and inclusion in university curriculums. Therefore, "the Canon, a word religious in its origins, has become a choice among texts struggling with one another for survival, whether you interpret the choice as being made by dominant social groups, institutions of education, traditions of criticism, or, as I do, by late-coming authors who feel themselves chosen by particular ancestral figures".[22] Undoubtedly, the operation of power and discourse behind the canon formation should also be taken into consideration.

Now that rewriting literary history from a new perspective must take into account the issue of canon formation and reformation, we have to admit objectively that any histories of world literature and any anthologies of world masterpieces produced in the Western context are apparently marked with a sort of "Eurocentrism" or "West-centrism", indicating that strong theoretical discourses deliberately overlook less influential discourses. This raises another question: Does the history of twentieth-century Chinese literature produced in the Chinese context have another shortcoming as well, such as over-emphasizing the political and ideological movements at the expense of ignoring the reader's reception? I think the answer should be yes. So it is not surprising that some young scholars tried several years ago to "rank" twentieth-century Chinese writers in a new way, and another group of young critics in recent years have even tried to remove those "established" writers who became well-known by various illegal or even evil means from the canonical writers' group.[23] In my view, no matter what their motivation, at least one positive point should be recognized: After the impact of such theories and cultural trends as postmodernism, aesthetics of reception and New Historicism, literary historiography has been demystified, and the narrowness of the established literary canon and the power behind it have been questioned. As a result, all the well-cultivated and well-trained reader-interpreters have the right to participate in canon formation and reformation. But such formation and reformation must be based on a certain theoretical perspective and profound understanding of what has already been done by other domestic researchers preceding us as well as by our foreign colleagues, otherwise any perfunctory conclusion based only on one's subjective impressions and perceptions without deep meditation cannot help reform the literary canon and rewrite literary history. On the contrary, some mediocre writers who have almost been lost from readers' memories might well be "highlighted" again, and they will be included among the canonical writers through the other channel. For from the perspective of literary experience and reception studies, even the critical negation of a certain writer will also help him become critically received, thereby paving the way for him to be included among the canonical writers or recorded in literary history. Undoubtedly, great writers might well be incompatible with their contemporaries, but they will definitely be "rediscovered" by later literary historiographers or researchers. Since those mediocre writers are no longer mentioned, why should we critics spend so much time calling for their return? Let them be forgotten by history, for history is always the best instrument to help select the best writers for inclusion in the canon.

4

The Popularization of English and the "Decolonization" of Chinese Critical Discourse

Of all the major international languages, English is undoubtedly the most popular and influential, not only in academic research circles in the East and West, North and South, but also in foreign trade, business, entertainment, and even in people's daily lives throughout the world. Since we are now in an era of globalization or transnational capitalism, the ability to communicate in English is becoming even more essential. The Western influence on Chinese literature since the beginning of the twentieth century has come about largely through the translation from English. Since the start of China's economic reform and openness to the outside world, English has become more and more attractive, and even indispensable, to young people at work and at play, and it is now the most popular foreign language used and taught in China. Many people, especially scientists, welcome the use of English as the primary means of communicating with the international community and popularizing their research results, but a few, especially scholars of old-fashioned humanistic orientation adhering to traditional Chinese culture, are worried about the possibility that the popularity of English might well do harm to China's national and cultural identity and even "colonize" Chinese literary criticism.[1] This chapter is an attempt to respond to the "decolonization" fears in Chinese scholarly and cultural circles.

POPULARIZATION OF ENGLISH IN THE CONTEXT OF GLOBALIZATION

In the current era of global and transnational capitalism, English has been playing an increasingly important role in Chinese scientific research and intellectual life, which finds particular embodiment in the recent widespread use of the Internet. English language and literature in the West have been subjected to the strong impact of cultural studies. The same is now happening in the critical circles of China's mainland. Some Chinese scholars fear that the rise of cultural studies actually sounds the death knell for canonical literature and traditional literary studies,[2] while others welcome it so that traditional elitist literary canon can be enlarged and reformed.[3] It is true that cultural studies has, in recent years, been introduced and discussed in Chinese critical circles along with postcolonialism or postcoloniality,[4] which came to the fore with the winding down of the heated discussion on postmodernism or postmodernity in the Chinese context in the latter part of the 1980s. Undoubtedly, cultural studies, a recent phenomenon in the English-speaking world, poses a severe challenge to elite culture and canonical literature. It is, to a large extent, a symbol of the linguistic hegemony of the US, whose political influence and economic power have exerted a profound influence on the English language itself. The so-called "Americanisms" are examples of this. So to deal with the popularization of English without referring to the prevalence of cultural studies is to not understand the "decolonization" of Chinese cultural and critical discourse. Any cultural or literary phenomenon, either from the East or West, could be read as a "text" from an international perspective. Similarly, any culture or literature, if it is to communicate and be examined in the broadest international context, has no choice but to function by means of English. This is a paradox for Chinese scholars of postcolonial studies: On the one hand, they intend to decolonize Chinese culture and critical discourse so as to defend and preserve the Chinese national and cultural identity; on the other hand, in order to communicate more effectively with the international scholarship—or more exactly, with Western scholarship—they have to publish their research results in English, the truly international language of today's scholars.

Cultural studies is also being discussed extensively in Hong Kong and Taiwan at the moment. As in the Western context, cultural studies in these societies does not point to traditional elitist culture, but rather to contemporary and even popular culture, including mass media and consumer culture. On the other hand, as far as the scope of cultural studies research is concerned, it no doubt includes the following aspects:

First, there is ethnic studies, with its focus on postcolonial and diasporic writing and criticism. This includes critical studies of such postcolonial theorists as Edward Said, whose theoretical doctrine is characterized by his critique and construction of "Orientalism", and by both ideological and disciplinary critique of this constructed concept; Gayatri Spivak, whose academic career and critical practice are informed by Derridean deconstruction and feminist postcolonial cultural politics of the Third World intellectuals; and Homi Bhabha, whose postcolonial criticism is characterized by the hybridization of national and cultural identity. With the deepening of the postcolonial debate, Bhabha's theory is becoming more and more attractive, especially among Third World critics and scholars whose critical focus is on the question of national identity and diaspora.[5]

Second, there is area studies, with its focus on the politics, economies, laws, histories, and cultures of some specific regions in an interdisciplinary manner; comprehensive studies of the Asian and Pacific regions are an example. Within this framework, such important issues as globalization and anti-Imperialist strategy are largely addressed. The recent Asian financial crisis, for example, is one among many other elements that are viewed as a direct consequence of economic and financial globalization. As far as our own research areas in the humanities and social sciences are concerned, I hold that cultural globalization, as a direct consequence of economic globalization, might well affect us in positive and negative ways. Its positive effect is that it enables our cultural industry and academic research to be manipulated by the rules of a market economy rather than by government intervention, thereby linking economic construction to cultural construction more closely. Its negative aspect lies in its making the production of elite culture or non-market-oriented cultural production more and more difficult, as a result of which a new sort of hierarchy is formed. In the current Chinese context, two dangerous trends should be brought to attention: First, the unremitting advocacy of cultural globalization in an attempt to use it to replace localization will certainly cause Chinese culture to lose its national identity; second, over-emphasizing cultural localization and rejecting all influences of foreign culture, compounded with a hostile attitude toward globalization, may well lead to another type of harmful cultural nationalism if it is pushed to the extremes. The latter will most probably set back China's international cultural and academic exchange and even prove detrimental to its economic construction.

The third aspect is gender studies, with its focus on female writing and women studies. This is characterized by shifting the attention on feminist cultural politics to emphasizing the importance of women's physiological and biological nature rather than their antagonistic position in a multicultural context. In this respect, women's cultural identity is reconstructed as a doubly marginalized force moving from the periphery to the centre, finally reconstructing a new female critical discourse different from that of the male-centred one. In recent years, along with the flourishing of female writing in China, feminist criticism and women studies are becoming more attractive to both male and female scholars.

The fourth aspect is mass media studies, with its focus on such popular cultural forms as film, television, advertising enterprises, Internet culture and writing, and other types of cultural industry; this is what cultural studies scholars are most concerned about. In the face of the impact made by the non-elite-oriented cultural studies, canonical literature and elite culture face a severe challenge. The popularity of the Internet and the Web has raised a stronger challenge against fictive writing and even traditional movies and television shows. The domain of literary creation and literary criticism has become narrower. Quite a few literary scholars and critics are worried about the future of literature in the new millennium.

Such is my understanding of the situation concerning cultural studies, both in the West and in China. I should say that all these aspects of cultural studies could be achieved by means of the popularization of English or the strengthening of the English linguistic hegemony. This is an inevitable consequence of the era of globalization, in which everybody feels tempted or pressured to learn to read and write in English, and no one can avoid being confronted with the spread of the English language if he/she does not want to isolate himself/herself from the international community. Thus, some might pose the question: How should we preserve our national and cultural identity in the face of the impact of English?

Obviously, in the context of globalization and transnational capitalism, scholars all agree that English functions as a new Imperial agent, without which one cannot keep abreast of recent advances in international scientific and scholarly research. With the popularization of English, cultural and national identity issues have attracted the attention of more and more scholars internationally who do not work exclusively in their own countries or regions. As Bhabha contends in his theory of hybridity or hybridization, globalization has increasingly obscured national and cultural identity. One person, whether at the centre (the First World) or periphery (the Third World), could function both at the centre and at the periphery—as happens with transnational corporations that have no fixed headquarters or central power and cannot be controlled by any one national government. This is true of many scholars from the Oriental and Third World countries, including China. This transnational identity even blurs these scholars' linguistic identities, as a result of which English becomes their only means of communicating with each other. On the one hand, scholars in China's humanities and social sciences take pains to introduce the most recent development in Western academic research so as to renew traditional Chinese scholarship; on the other hand, they have to write their most important academic works in English and publish them in some leading international journals or with internationally prestigious university presses, in an attempt to have them recognized by their Western and international colleagues. This is a significant phenomenon in Chinese cultural studies.

Therefore, as the most commonly used international language in the so-called "global village", the influence of English is spreading, especially in those countries where the modernizing process occurs at an accelerated pace.[6] In these countries, to be modernized actually means to be Westernized in one way or another. Contemporary China's openness to the outside world and economic reform encourage the popularization of English. All major universities, both at national and provincial levels, have set up departments of English or foreign languages, with the teaching of English as the major activity. Teaching of other foreign languages is either developing slowly or on the decline. Moreover, all university students, both at undergraduate and graduate levels, tend to take English as a compulsory course, no matter what subjects they are doing research in. In writing their PhD dissertations, candidates from all fields are encouraged to use the original references in a foreign language, usually in English, if they are to pass their dissertation defence. All academic researchers or scholars are required to pass an examination in at least one foreign language, usually English, before they can apply for promotion.[7] In almost all of China's urban high schools (and even primary schools in some big cities), students are required to take a course in a foreign language, usually English, before they can get their graduate diplomas and degrees. Apart from its use in China's universities and research institutes, English is also widely used in all commercial trades or fields of learning, and even in consumer and advertising enterprises. There is no doubt that the teaching of English in China is flourishing (as is reflected in the income of English teachers). This is a signal that China's academic research is becoming increasingly internationalized or globalized, which would be impossible without the medium of English. This is not only a fact of life but a historical necessity in China. So, in the era of globalization, whether we like it or not, we have to know English; without it, we can hardly survive and work successfully in the contemporary world.

"DECOLONIZING" CHINESE CULTURE AND CRITICAL DISCOURSE?

The advent of globalization enables China to establish an irreplaceable, unique presence in the world. As a direct consequence of economic and financial globalization, cultural globalization has affected China's intellectual life and literary and critical discourse. It is incumbent on scholars to find themselves a place in the process of (cultural) globalization. Undoubtedly, cultural globalization has enabled us to converse with the international community and scholarship more conveniently as more and more scholars master the English language and obtain easy access to the Internet. Within the field of literary theory and criticism in China, some scholars, including myself, spend much time and energy translating the most recent research works on critical theory and cultural studies published in the West into Chinese, in an attempt to influence and renew contemporary Chinese literary theory and criticism. Since the beginning of the 1980s, such Western critical theories and cultural and academic trends as formalism, New Criticism, phenomenology, structuralism, existentialism, psychoanalysis of Freudianism, poststructuralism, hermeneutics, the aesthetics of reception, New Historicism, postmodernism, postcolonialism and cultural studies have entered the literary and critical scene in contemporary China one after another, exerting a strong influence on Chinese literary theory and criticism as well as literary scholarship. The major writings of almost all Western modernist literary masters are now available in Chinese. These have had a greater influence on a number of young writers than many Chinese writers' works. But on the other hand, there have also appeared some unhealthy tendencies; some young scholars whose theoretical and English foundation is rather shallow chase after the dominant intellectual fashions, often misusing critical terms borrowed from the West in their critical and theoretical works to such an extent that not only ordinary readers but even specialists in the field cannot understand what they are saying. Obviously, this is not a good sign for China's literary theory and scholarship to carry out dialogues with the international literary scholarship on an equitable level. Therefore, it is not surprising that these Chinese scholars and critics would rather stick to the traditional Chinese cultural identity and critical conventions which are uncontaminated by foreign influences. To these scholars, China is a major literary country with its own long tradition of literary theory and criticism that now does not utter its own voice in international critical and theoretical debates. They complain that Chinese literary theorists and scholars do not even have their own critical discourse.[8] Thus, the whole country has become a country without voice or critical discourse. Out of their concern for the construction or reconstruction of China's critical and theoretical discourse, these scholars call for the establishment of their own critical and theoretical discourse and view it as one of the postcolonial strategies in the process of China's cultural "decolonization". In comparative literature studies, the call for setting up a "Chinese School" is once again reaching people's ears.[9] It finds particular embodiment in several conferences on literary theory and comparative literature and in critical articles published in certain journals.[10] Obviously, to those scholars, globalization and foreign influences are inevitably opposed to the development of Chinese literature and the construction of Chinese critical discourse and are thus the main causes of the "colonization" of Chinese culture and its critical discourse. And the agent of such an influence is no doubt the popularization of English.

If we were to consider this phenomenon carefully, we would realize that whether or not Chinese culture and critical discourse become "colonized" depends on various factors. Some people hold that the popularization of English is responsible for the overall Westernization of Chinese literary theory and criticism in the past two decades, from content to discourse, since many of the theoretical doctrines and cultural and academic trends have been introduced in China by means of English. As a result, Chinese culture has lost its own national identity, and critics have lost their own discourse and even their voice in international theoretical debates since they cannot speak in English. Others think it is necessary to realize the decolonization of Chinese culture by means of a "Chinese School" in comparative literature studies, which used to be attractive in the 1980s when comparative literature as a discipline was "rediscovered" after a long period of "silence" but which is now, in my opinion, nothing but a reversal of the old-fashioned "Eurocentrism" or "West-centrism"; that is, the so-called "China-centrism". They obviously have every right to raise the question of whether having a grasp of English serves as a measure of whether or not one is noble-minded and learned. In contrast, in the West, especially in the US, few people speak Chinese, let alone understand the profound spirit of Chinese culture and philosophical thinking. In order to go abroad for advanced studies, Chinese students or scholars have to first pass their English proficiency examinations; however, those Western experts working in China are not necessarily obliged to learn how to speak Chinese. They are usually accompanied by young Chinese interpreters when they are doing business or on a tour. Is this not an imbalance in cultural exchange? We cannot deny the truth of all these observations, at least as things stand now, but we need to look at them more closely and more analytically.

We should acknowledge that these scholars and critics have reasons to worry about the penetrating power and hegemony of English in the international community and the "colonization" of Chinese culture and theoretical and critical discourse. Actually, since the beginning of the 1990s, along with the introduction of postmodernism and subsequently postcolonialism, there has been a "postist fad" (*houxue re*), especially a "postcolonial fad", used as an antagonistic strategy in the struggle against the so-called Western neo-colonialist cultural penetration in the Chinese context. Many Chinese "conservatives" do think that Chinese culture and literary discourse have been "colonized" since the turn of the century, or more exactly, since the May 4th Movement, which marked the beginning of new Chinese literature and culture that have been responsible for such a "colonized" state as is shown in the Chinese language which has been more or less "Europeanized" or "Westernized". It is true that Chinese culture and literature were almost free of any Western influence before that time; it is also true that after China opened its doors to the outside world, Western academic thoughts and cultural theories flooded into China, exerting a strong influence on modern Chinese culture and literary discourse. In this respect, Lu Xun's principle

55

of "grabbism" (*nalai zhuyi*) is best known and has been most influential till today. Of course, it is both a good thing and a bad thing: It is good for Chinese culture and literature to move away from isolation and get into the mainstream of world culture and literature, but it is bad that the introduction of these trends and theories has obscured the national identity of Chinese culture, which has had a long and splendid tradition but is now being "colonized". This dilemma confronting the Chinese scholars is becoming more evident, making us increasingly worried about the future of Chinese culture and literary criticism. In my view, however, to solve the problem and continue to communicate with the outside world will by no means belittle Chinese culture or deconstruct its literary discourse, for it is a necessary sacrifice in the course of modernizing Chinese culture and literature.

Here, I want to argue that it is necessary to adopt a dialectical attitude toward those complicated phenomena in Chinese culture and literature. The popularization of English should not necessarily give rise to the "colonization" of Chinese culture and literary and critical discourse. We have taken great pains in the past few years to translate Western culture and literature into Chinese by means of English, which has certainly helped us to have a better understanding of the world and contributed to the flourishing of Chinese literature and culture. But along with the elevation of China's position in the international community, the aesthetic value and profound thinking of Chinese culture and literature have been gaining recognition by Western sinologists as well as the broad reading public. In this sense, the popularization of English will in turn help us to introduce the very spirit of Chinese culture and literature to the outside world since English is still the most popular international language in academic research as well as in daily communication. Scientists have already taken the lead in this respect. It is time for us in the humanities and social sciences to do likewise.[11] In the case of comparative literature, one of the most international disciplines in China today, if we recognize that the first stage of comparative literature studies in China is characterized by influence-reception studies, especially how Western literature has influenced Chinese literature, then the second stage into which we are about to move will be characterized by paying more attention to how Chinese literature and culture is disseminated in the world.[12] In this way, publishing our research results in English is all the more necessary. We have only just started to do so. So it is certainly good for us to introduce the rich Chinese cultural heritage and its excellent literary works to the world by means of English so that Western people will know what China is really like rather than what it appears to be, judging from books written out of ignorance, which misread and misconstruct China and its people. In this way, to emphasize cultural decolonization does not necessarily mean writing off the popularization of English, for Chinese culture has never been totally "colonized", although the country was once partly colonized.[13] On the contrary, only by raising the level of our English proficiency in an all-round way can we communicate with the international community more efficiently. So the popularization of English is not an impediment to the construction of China's literary and critical discourse at all. With the help of English, we can only understand the world better and do a great deal of good for the construction of Chinese critical discourse.

THE FUNCTION OF ENGLISH IN CONSTRUCTING CHINESE CRITICAL DISCOURSE

It is true that we are now in an age of globalization, both economically and culturally. Whether we in China like it or not, it is a historical necessity beyond anyone's expectation or resistance. Since China has officially entered the (socialist) market economy system, it is already in the process of globalization. It cannot escape the relentless "law of the jungle". In this respect, it can be predicted that English will play a much more important role in people's lives as the world today becomes smaller and smaller. We all live in a huge "global village", in which we can easily communicate with each other, exchanging views on different subjects and cooperating in undertaking huge joint ventures. If we all speak our own languages exclusively, it would be chaotic, given the hundreds of languages in the world. We certainly have to agree upon one or two languages spoken by comparatively larger communities from different countries to serve as our major means of communication. Given this, we cannot but choose English as the most convenient means of international communication. In order for our research results to be recognized by international scholars, we have to write our major works in English and translate our most important ideas into English—which disappoints conservative scholars. They might well ask why all the prestigious international journals are published in English instead of Chinese, which is spoken by the largest number of people in the world as their mother tongue, and why the members of the Nobel Committee for Literature are not able to read the original Chinese literary works.[14] It is true that China is one of the largest countries in the world with the largest population; that is, the Chinese-speaking population is the largest in the world. Yet this statistic does not make it possible for people all over the world to communicate with each other in Chinese now. It is obviously unrealistic, not only because the Chinese government cannot afford to support all those who are interested in learning the language even though there might be many people from different countries who intend to take Chinese courses, but, more importantly, the Chinese language is one of the most difficult languages to master, even for many Chinese intellectuals. Furthermore, Chinese characters are not compatible with the internationally prevailing linguistic system or the Internet. Since English is already the most popular language used by people from many countries either as their native tongue or official language or the first foreign language, why should we not use it at least for the moment? We cannot help but realize—though reluctantly—that it is our only choice; without English, we would end up isolating ourselves again from the international scholarship.

It is understandable that within our own fields of literary criticism and cultural studies, scholars are very much worried about the possible "colonization" of Chinese culture and literary and critical discourse. But their strategy should not be to prevent people from studying English. If we have a good grasp of English, we would be able to participate in international academic discussions and have a "voice", although in a non-native tongue. But if we do not study English—as was the practice on the mainland during the years from 1949 to 1976—Chinese scholars would not have any "voice" on any international academic occasion and would be forced to interact among themselves or with a limited number of sinologists.

Here, I should mention one existing fact. Learning Chinese is becoming more and more popular, both in China and elsewhere.[15] More and more foreigners come to China not only to learn to speak the language in order to do business with China, but also to understand the very spirit of Chinese culture and literature. What revelations have been made from such an existing phenomenon? In the past, such a situation would be impossible. Those who were interested in doing business with China came only to learn the Chinese language, by means of which they could easily negotiate with their Chinese partners. But now Western intellectuals admit that Chinese culture could enrich their own culture.

So more and more young Western people are coming to China not only to learn the language but also to work on their MA and even PhD studies after attaining their first degrees. But in their preliminary stage of study, in order to make them interested in Chinese culture and literature, we must lecture on these topics in English. Eventually, they find that something is missing in learning Chinese culture and literature through the medium of English, and they want to read and appreciate Chinese literature and culture directly in Chinese.[16] I dare say that in the future, along with the rapid growth of China's economy and the steady development of Chinese culture and literature, the Chinese language will become increasingly important and popular in international communication. If that is a likely realization in the future, then we should attach more importance to the study of English now, for it will help us to popularize Chinese culture and literature rather than "colonize" them. It is then absolutely unnecessary to launch a movement to "decolonize" Chinese culture and literary and critical discourse in an age of globalization.

CHAPTER 5

Translatology: Toward a Scientific Discipline

Translation studies has been developing steadily both in China and the West, although it has always been challenged and even repressed by other traditional and "orthodox" disciplines or branches of learning, both in social sciences and the humanities. Scholars in this field have indeed spent much time and effort discussing or debating about whether translation is an art or a science but with no definite conclusion. Since many practising translators, especially those of literature, maintain that translation is an art, translation theory is naturally based on the experiences accumulated in such an artistic practice. Doing translation studies is, therefore, nothing but summing up the very experience of translation practice. And it is said in turn to guide translation practice. This is certainly true to some extent. But if we want to justify the existence of translation studies as a scientific discipline or a branch of learning, like literary studies or art history and theory, such a superficial definition is obviously far from enough. In my view, if we want to relocate translation as well as translation studies in the current context of globalization, we should first of all distinguish between the two: The former appeals to a practical technique backed up by a comprehensive range of knowledge and frequent practice, while the latter itself functions as a branch of learning, or a branch of human knowledge characterized by theoretical discussion and empirical research in a thorough way. Although translation theory is supposed to guide translation practice, along with its increasing maturity, it has become more and more autonomous and is moving farther and farther away from translation practice like other independent disciplines. Along with the advent of the age of globalization, it seems that translation will become obsolete since world cultures are becoming more and more homogenized and we can easily get access to any information in English on the Internet. However, translation is still necessary as long as there are human beings who communicate with each other in different languages and with different cultural backgrounds.

Thus, translation studies should continue to occupy a place in human knowledge and play a vital role in the future if we try to relocate it in today's context.

TRANSLATION AT PRESENT: LITERAL RENDITION OR CULTURAL INTERPRETATION?

Although different theorists have different opinions about the definition and function of translation, translation is, in the final analysis, absolutely necessary to our daily life and interpersonal communication, without which we can only isolate ourselves from the outside world, especially in the current age of globalization. In such a vast "global village", people from different countries with different cultural backgrounds and even from different continents can easily communicate with each other by various means. The most frequently used means is undoubtedly *language*. Thus, translation is a technique in which the meaning in one language is rendered into another language, and vice versa. But the issue of how to produce an ideal and most relevant translation has been heatedly discussed ever since translation came into being. Almost all translators try to approach the original meaning expressed in the source language in the process of translation, and translation theorists have tried to develop a sort of theory which can be applied as a universally recognized guiding principle for practising translators. One of the recent examples finds particular embodiment in Eugene Nida's practical strategy; that is, his concept of "dynamic equivalence", in which the translator "aims at complete naturalness of expression, and tries to relate the receptor to modes of behavior relevant within the context of his own culture".[1] This famous sentence is often quoted by Chinese scholars of translation studies as a canonical principle although it is no longer mentioned in Western translation studies circles. Obviously, Nida has long realized that complete equivalence is impossible and unnecessary, so he tries to find a relatively relevant way to represent the original meaning expressed in the source language by putting forward this "dynamic equivalence" as he understands the dynamic function of the translator. It is true that after the poststructuralist deconstructive effort made in human knowledge, we have to realize that no translator can affirm that he has already grasped the truth; what he may have grasped is only approaching the truth. That is why translators of different generations spend much time re-translating some canonical literary works so as to meet the demands of the reading public in different periods of time.

It should be pointed out that Nida's theoretical concept is still on the linguistic level although he has more or less touched upon some aspects of culture. But the most recent example in exploring a "relevant translation" perhaps finds particular embodiment in Jacques Derrida's speech delivered in 1998 at the fifteenth annual seminar of the Assises de la Traduction litteraire a Arles (ATLAS). Although Derrida cannot be regarded as a translator as he seldom practises translation, he is indeed universally recognized as a great theorist of cultural translation, or a translator in the postmodern sense. What he means by translation is not the traditional "word for word" rendition on the linguistic level, but rather the "sense for sense" translation or interpretation on the cultural level. Thanks to his deconstructive strategy in undermining traditional philosophy and liberating literature, these two disciplines of learning are interconnected. As a result, he himself has become more influential in literary theory than in philosophy.

Derrida, like other theorists of postmodernism, does not believe in the legitimacy and authenticity of an absolutely relevant translation, for everything is in existence relative to something else. So to him, as well as his interpreters, the idea of a "relevant" translation is by no means "new in translation theory, even if it has been subject to varying formulations, particularly over the last three centuries".[2] Although a completely "relevant" translation is impossible, a relatively "relevant" translation could be achieved if the translator tries his best to do so. From Derrida's theory, we have already seen a shift of focus in (relevant) translation from "purely" linguistic rendition to dynamic and cultural interpretation and representation. In this sense, we should say that Derrida himself is more a theoretic and cultural interpreter (translator) than a translator in its traditional sense. He likes the word, but to him, the word appears as "Word" rather than its literal meaning. To him, it functions both linguistically as well as culturally: "As for the word (for the word will be my theme)—neither grammar nor lexicon hold an interest for me—I believe I can say that if I love the word, it is only in the body of its idiomatic singularity, that is, where a passion for translation comes to lick it as a flame or an amorous tongue might: approaching as closely as possible while refusing at the last moment to threaten or to reduce, to consume or to consummate, leaving the other body intact but not without causing the other to appear—on the very brink of this refusal or withdrawal—and after having aroused or excited a desire for the idiom, for the unique body of the other, in the flame's flicker or through a tongue's caress."[3]

Undoubtedly, different scholars or translators explore the issue of relevant translation from their own angles. I myself once practised some translation, but mostly theoretical translation and cultural interpretation. So my perspective is certainly that of culture although I always hold that literal translation in certain contexts is absolutely essential to represent the very meaning of the original text in a faithful way, especially in the translation of scientific documents. In literary translation, however, it is of utmost importance to represent the very subtle meaning between the lines and even behind the lines. Literary works usually imply very subtle cultural and aesthetic connotations that are untranslatable if the translator only adheres to the superficial fidelity on the linguistic level. Thus, equivalence on the verbal level or sentence level is sometimes impossible and unnecessary, for according to this standard, Lin Shu—one of the pioneering figures of China's literary translation—cannot even be seen as a translator, although his important role in the history of modern translated Chinese literature is generally recognized. To an excellent translator, therefore, to be faithful in spirit and in style is much better than to be faithful merely in words and sentences. Hence, I would like to re-emphasize that it is necessary to redefine translation in a new context, for along with the deepening of cultural studies, more and more scholars have realized that translation has much to do with culture. Therefore, it is possible to do translation studies in the broader context of cultural studies as translation touches on at least two or more different cultures beyond the boundary of languages. It is not just a matter of "pure" literal rendition of the meaning of the original (source) language in another (target) language.

According to the standard of an ideal translation, we should recognize that "no translation strategy can be linked deterministically to a textual effect, theme, cultural discourse, ideology, or institution. Such linkages are contingent upon the cultural and political situation in which the translator is produced. Literalizing strategies have actually been put to contrary uses in the history of translation."[4] Therefore, I want to point out that in today's context of global cultural communication, what we need most is to understand the subtlety of foreign cultures so as to communicate most effectively with people of those cultural traditions. Thus, "a relevant translation would therefore be, quite simply, a 'good' translation, a translation that does what one expects of it, in short, a version that performs its mission, honors its debt and does its job or its duty while inscribing in the receiving language the more *relevant* equivalent for an original, the language that is *the most* right, appropriate, pertinent, adequate, opportune, pointed, univocal, idiomatic, and so on".[5]

But how can we reach such a high standard of "relevant translation"? Derrida does not stop deconstructing the established convention: "On the other hand, a relevant translation is assumed, rightly or wrongly, to be better than a translation that is not relevant. A relevant translation is held, rightly or wrongly, to be the best translation possible. The teleological definition of translation, the definition of the essence that is realized in translation, is therefore implicated in the definition of a relevant translation. The question, 'What is a relevant translation?' would return to the question, 'What is translation?' or, 'What should a translation be?' And the question, 'What should a translation be?' implies, as if synonymously, 'What should the best possible translation be?'"[6] Although he tries to give a standard for a relevant translation or best translation, he actually indicates that such a standard itself is uncertain and still a moot point.

Here, I would like to further Derrida's effort and offer my own definition of translation once again.[7] In my view, translation in today's sense should be both a linguistic rendition as well as a cultural interpretation, with more emphasis on the latter. Obviously, in today's context, someone who does not understand a foreign language like Lin Shu cannot be regarded as a translator. Nor could he/she do any practical translation work. But translation in today's context should shift its function from mere linguistic rendition to cultural interpretation. The former can be done by a translation machine, but the latter can only be accomplished by human beings, for only human beings can grasp most appropriately the very subtlety of culture and represent it in a most relevant way.

THE FUNCTION OF TRANSLATION
IN THE AGE OF GLOBALIZATION

We are obviously in an age of globalization, or what William Martin describes as an "electronic global village where, through the mediation of information and communication technologies, new patterns of social and cultural organization are emerging".[8] Such an information society has undoubtedly condensed the traditional concept of time and space, enabling people to communicate more directly and more easily. Whether we recognize it or not, globalization is an objective phenomenon, although it appears as a ghost-like spectre haunting our memories every now and then and influencing our cultural and intellectual life as well as our academic studies. Globalization is not something created by scholars, but rather an objective phenomenon in our daily life. Under the impact of globalization, the cultural and literary market has been shrinking. The humanities and social sciences are severely challenged by the overload of knowledge and information. On the other hand, the function of the English language is much more obvious: All scientific papers should be published in English if their authors intend to have them recognized by their international colleagues, and people from different parts of the world would rather communicate in English than in their own languages. In this way, English is playing an increasingly important role in such a global information society. We can easily get access to most of the information on the Internet by means of English. We can easily survive in the present era if we get access to information, and if we have a good command of English, we can get even more information. If we still believe that knowledge is strength, then in the age of globalization, information is power, and knowledge will become riches. In this sense, people might well raise this question: Since everybody communicates in English, of what use is translation? On the contrary, translation will be all the more necessary in such an age of globalization, although many people are learning to communicate directly in English so as to communicate more effectively with each other and avoid any misunderstanding. Scientists communicate in English as they do not want to have their scientific discoveries distorted or erroneously illustrated. So they need talented translators who can produce relevant translations which not only render the literal meaning of their papers, but also the very subtle nuances of the cultural aspects.

Obviously, globalization has marginalized the majority of people, with only 20 per cent of the world population directly benefiting from the globalization process. Economic globalization has given rise to cultural globalization in which Western, or specifically American, culture is imposing its values upon Third World culture. So some non-English-speaking people are very much worried about the possible "colonization" of their cultures and languages. What is then the function of translation in the age of globalization since cultures are becoming more and more homogenized? First of all, we should recognize that globalization gives rise to the interpenetrating processes of the universalization of particularism and the particularization of universalism.[9] That is, the impact of globalization is embodied at two poles: its effect travels from the West to the East and, at the same time, from the East to the West. Dialectically speaking, globalization has created linkages between different social and cultural phenomena, such as identities, social relationships and even institutions, and these linkages must be placed within a specific historical context.[10] Just as Gayatri Spivak correctly points out, it is true that in the age of globalization "all identities are irreducibly hybrid, inevitably instituted by the representation of performance as statement",[11] but new identities could be constructed or reconstructed in the new cultural context. Thus, communication between different societies, cultures and nations is becoming more and more frequent. But how can this communication be more effective? Undoubtedly by means of information exchanges in which language—or more specifically, the English language—plays the most important role. In this way, translation is all the more inevitable, functioning not only as a means of communication, but also as a means of cultural exchange and political strategy. It has gone far beyond the superficial level of linguistic aspects, so the research on translation should attach more importance to the cultural aspects of translation.

Let us now come back again to Derrida's speech at the ATLAS annual conference. As might be expected from an audience composed primarily of professional translators, the response to his lecture "was mixed, a range of variations between two extremes: on the one hand, the feeling that the lecture was provocative but too theoretical to be of practical value; on the other hand, the feeling that it was accessible and pertinent, indeed, an illuminating treatment of translation practices".[12] My understanding is like this: To those practising translators who only stick to the linguistic function of translation, his speech cannot serve as a guiding principle on how to do translation well, but to those whose horizon of knowledge has already been widened to include that of culture, his speech will certainly illuminate them in their cultural and theoretical construction so that they will most probably expand the domain of translation. As for scholars of translation studies, they are certainly encouraged to explore the very limits of relevant translation, both on the linguistic level as well as on the cultural level, from theoretical and disciplinary perspectives. Here, Derrida, as a deconstructionist both in theory and in practice, does not want to establish a principle; what he intends to do is to effectively create the possibility of approaching a relevant translation.

In dealing with the aspects of translation, Roman Jakobson once distinguished these three aspects: interlinguistic, intralinguistic, and intersemiotic.[13] His formalistic and structuralistic orientation in defining and positioning translation is very conspicuous. But I would add one more factor—intercultural translation—which will play a more and more important role in the age of globalization. I am of the opinion that although current cultural studies in the English-speaking world has exerted a strong influence on, or even severely challenged, literary studies, it should not necessarily influence translation studies as translation is first of all an issue of culture, hence translation studies is part of cultural studies. Even in the "global village" today, cultural communication and exchange should be attained by means of translation. So I hold that in the age of globalization, however marginalized literature and other cultural forms might be, translation will still occupy a vital place in our cultural and intellectual life as well as in our daily communication.

TOWARD A SCIENTIFIC AND INDEPENDENT DISCIPLINE

In view of the above, I think it is high time that we reposition our translation research, or translatology, as a scientific and independent discipline. Although the term "translatology" has not yet been legitimately and universally recognized as with other independent disciplines or branches of learning in the university curricula, it has been widely used among translation scholars, especially among European and American translation scholars. It is usually called the science of translation or translation scholarship. It is formed on the basis of translation practice, but does not necessarily serve to guide the latter since it is autonomous, with its own research domain, objects and methodology. It will not only contribute to translation practice where possible, but, more importantly, it will contribute to the construction of the humanities and social sciences at large. We should acknowledge that without translation practice, there is no way of establishing the discipline of translation scholarship. But unfortunately, due to the long-term over-emphasis on the pragmatic function of translation studies as a guide to translation practice, decision-makers, especially in China, have overlooked the legitimacy of translation studies or translatology as an independent discipline although translation research has been done separately in the fields of linguistics, applied linguistics and literary and cultural studies. What is even worse is that translated works, however theoretic, academic or valuable, are not regarded as scholarly works, while those produced on the basis of "translation", compilation and even plagiarism are viewed as "original", "creative" or "scholarly" works. It is indeed unfair and tragic.

Translatology should be regarded as an independent discipline, distinct from other disciplines such as linguistics and literary studies. Its recognition has already been demonstrated in the establishment of several departments of translation in a few Chinese universities both in the mainland and in Hong Kong. With quite a few scholarly publications and periodicals supporting its foundation and the development of teaching plans in university curricula, it is certainly maturing. With its unique characteristics, it is impossible to categorize translatology as strictly a humanities field if we take into consideration its linguistic aspects, aesthetic and cultural connotations and positivistic nature of research, nor should we simply include it in the social sciences only, for it still has the function of cultural interpretation and representation if we think of translation as an issue involving culture. In this way, translatology should be regarded as a marginal discipline like semiotics, anthropology and even psychology, for it has much to do with natural science (for instance, machine translation, developing new translation software, computer language, etc.), social science (for instance, the empirical study of translations, linguistic analysis of different translations, etc.) and the humanities (aesthetic appreciation of literary translations, comparative study of different versions of the same canonical literary work, etc.). All these should serve as the basis on which an independent discipline is established.

Obviously, as an independent discipline, translatology should have its own research objects and domain of research, as well as its own major methodology. In my view, translatology is a discipline or branch of learning with all the phenomena in translation practice and theory as its research objects. Its methodology should be pluralistic: both aesthetic (directed chiefly to literary translation) and empirical (directed chiefly to scientific translation and documentary translation) or something else. Concretely, translation studies should be done on the following three levels:

1. *On the level of comparative literature studies.* In the past dozen years, when translation studies was marginalized, quite a few comparatists, such as André Lefevere and Eugene Eoyang, conscientiously engaged in translation studies by comparing two, or more than two, forms of European and American literature beyond comparative studies, or between Chinese and Western literature. Their practice and theoretic exploration have paved the way for translation studies to become an independent discipline distinct from comparative literature studies.

2. *On the level of analyzing the linguistic aspects of translated texts.* If we say that the first level is characterized by dynamic interpretation and aesthetic representation, this second level is characterized by pure empirical or scientific research of translated texts. That is, we should return to the original text that manipulates the law of translation and covers the matter of translatability, for translation is nothing but a form.[14]

3. *On the level of cultural studies in the context of which translation studies is carried out in a theoretical and interpretive way.* It is true that cultural studies is known to be anti-institution and anti-theory, but its practice has proved that it is backed up by various post-modern theories characterized by the liberation of all the repressed marginal discourses, sub-cultures as well as sub-genres of literature. In this way, translation studies is part of cultural studies in its broad sense and could borrow methodologies from the latter.

Then one might well raise this question: Since interdisciplinary studies is characterized by the learnings of the twenty-first century, why should we isolate translatology from other disciplines? The answer is very simple: Translatology is more characteristic of interdisciplinariness than merely a discipline in its traditional sense. This is perhaps the very reason why we try to highlight translatology as an independent but scientific and marginal discipline in the age of globalization.

Translation Studies in the Context of Chinese-Western Comparative Culture Studies

Translation studies in China has actually been around since the Han Dynasty, but as China was an isolated country that was seldom open to the outside world during the past few centuries, great importance was not attached to translation studies until the turn of the last century, when Western academic works and literary writings flooded into China, making a strong impact on the rise of new Chinese literature (*xin wenxue*) marked by the May 4th Movement in 1919. Since then, translation has been regarded as being as important as creative writing, especially by those who strongly advocate the "overall Westernization" (*quanpan xihua*) of culture.[1] Yan Fu (1854–1921) was well-known for his important but controversial principle on translation, especially literary translation from foreign languages into Chinese—that is, faithfulness, expressiveness and elegance (*xin, da, ya*)—which has provoked endless debates since. But in my opinion, in contrast with the rapid development of translation theories and translation studies toward a scientific discipline and empirical approach in the West, Chinese translation studies has long been on the level of translation review or translation criticism, and far from the establishment of a theoretical system of Chinese translation studies in the present context of cultural studies.[2] Nor has it reached the international level of the empirically oriented translation studies. So in the present chapter, I will first of all start by questioning Yan's principle, from which I will address some theoretical issues from the perspective of Chinese–Western comparative culture studies in the context of which translation studies in China could be done.

RECONSTRUCTING AN IDEAL CRITERION
FOR LITERARY TRANSLATION

Chinese scholars now often argue about whether translation is a science or an art; such a question is especially controversial for literary translation in China due to the fact that most of the scholars of translation studies are engaged in the study of literature or are themselves translators of literary works. Generally, people always think that translation is regarded as a science by Western scholars, whereas to most Chinese scholars, translation is viewed rather as an art by appealing to its technical procedure.[3] They usually start their argument with a quotation taken from Eugene Nida: "Translating consists in reproducing in the receptor language the closest natural equivalent of the source language message, first in terms of meaning, and secondly in terms of style."[4] But to my knowledge, in its recent development, translation studies has a tendency of combining the two factors, especially in the translation of literature. According to André Lefevere who was himself both a translator as well as a comparatist, "the translation of literature [takes] place not in a vacuum in which two languages meet but, rather, in the context of all the traditions of the two literatures. It also takes place when writers and their translators meet an encounter in which at least one of the parties is a human being, made of flesh and blood and provided with an agenda of his or her own. Translators mediate between literary traditions, and they do so with some goal in mind, other than that of 'making the original available' in a neutral, objective way. Translations are not produced under perfect laboratory conditions. Originals are indeed made available, but on the translators' term, even if these terms happen to produce the closest literal (faithful) translation."[5] Here, the idea that the translation of literature is both scientific (objective and faithful) and aesthetic (dynamic and creative) is clearly described, so to appeal only to pure faithfulness within the domain of literature is far from enough. We cannot still maintain that translation in the West is just regarded as a science but as an art in China. Such binary opposition as that of the "either/or" mode of thinking will obviously prevent us from setting up an ideal paradigm for both Western and Chinese translators as well as translation scholars. We should transcend to a higher level and reflect on the established criterion for translation in a broader cultural context; that is, a translator of literature is actually involved in the translation of culture.

In the current Chinese debate on the criterion for literary translation, Yan Fu's principle of an ideal criterion for literary translation is always cited, discussed or even questioned before substantial exploration of the issue starts, partly because it is very difficult to reach such a perfect level as required by Yan. Scholars tend to suspect the existence of a criterion, partly because the definition of his three points of translation is so indeterminate that it often arouses debates or controversies, and more importantly because in the literary translation of a foreign language—or more specifically, a Western language—into Chinese or vice versa, it is almost impossible to meet Yan's ideal criterion. That is, the three points in the principle cannot all be realized at the same time. The realization of this three-point criterion is relative, or more precisely, occurs on different levels. Of course, many discussions are still carried out about the technical problems, such as how to translate one sentence into idiomatic Chinese or how to find the best equivalent to render the exact meaning of the original. In this way, such debates are certainly endless and insignificant if we intend to broaden our scope of view. To solve this problem, I think it necessary to rethink and even reconstruct Yan's principle before we put forward our new paradigm.

But what on earth does Yan mean by "faithfulness, expressiveness and elegance"? Can we transcend ourselves to a higher level beyond such a technical question? In this sense, I would offer my own explanation or reinterpretation of Yan's three points in a broader cultural context.

By "faithfulness", Yan means that a good translation should certainly be as faithful to the original text as possible. Although it is not so clearly defined, to my mind, it simply means that the translator should first of all read the original text closely, between the lines and even behind the lines, so that nothing subtle escapes his eyes. Here, we come across a problem on the cultural level. As we know, every culture exists in relation to other cultures as different cultures are characteristically different. Since Euro-American cultures, although in the Western context, differ greatly in many aspects, Western culture as a whole must have a more striking difference compared to Chinese culture which obviously belongs to an entirely different tradition. In this way, in reading a literary text, misreading cannot but occur, some of which would lead to cultural innovation and even cultural construction, which can easily find embodiment in the reception of Western theories in China since the May 4th period. For instance, the critical and creative reception of Nietzsche in that period is interesting enough to emphasize his "transvaluating everything" characteristic rather than his concept of the superman. Thus, Nietzsche's theory was certainly popular among such major revolutionary writers as Lu Xun, Guo Moruo and Mao Dun at the time.[6] But after the founding of the People's Republic of China, Nietzsche's theory was forbidden and severely attacked as one of the typical bourgeois ideologies heralding fascism. We cannot say that the translator has failed to translate Niezsche's theory in a precise way although many of his works have been translated from English, and by those whose English is far from perfect. But it is his concept of the superman rather than the characteristic of "transvaluating everything" that is regarded as the essence of Nietzsche's theory. Thus, cultural misreading is more serious than just a literal misunderstanding. For, as Fred Inglis points out, "Ideology may be something of which you are persuaded by other people against your better judgement or even without your noticing. Ideology may also be no more than a name to describe the ramshackle, bits-and-pieces way in which you have nailed together a framework of beliefs in order to keep out the political weather. More typically, ideology may be the term of abuse you keep on hand to describe the virulent fixity and argumentative completeness with which other people hold beliefs different to yours (and, what is more, use them to attack you victoriously)."[7] So even to realize a relative faithfulness still means writing off any misreading (here it is more critical than a misunderstanding) and subjective construction. Thus, faithfulness should be the first element of importance; translation should be carried out without inserting the translator's own subjective ideological tendency although he/she might be for/against the original author's idea.

Similarly, Yan's second point in his criterion is "expressiveness" or fluency, by which he intends to emphasize the fluent way of rendering the translation in the target language on the basis of a correct understanding of the original text. Since there can be no absolute faithfulness to the original text, expressiveness can only be reached in a relative way. And there are two premises: Be faithful to the original text both in content and in style and render the translation according to the convention of the target language. That is, for many of Yan's interpreters, this should be as important as the first point since the translated version is for readers who have little or even no knowledge of the source language. If the translated version is not readable, it is obviously a failure from the reader's point of view. But still, there are some writers and scholars, such as Lu Xun, who would rather stick to faithfulness at the expense of expressiveness, and from which he even launched strong ideological attacks on many of his contemporaries.[8] Thus, the second point of Yan's principle is still uncertain and controversial although most of the scholars do think that expressiveness is equal to readability on the basis of faithfulness.

If we do not negate the validity of the first two points, then the third one is all the more problematic, for according to Yan, "elegance" by no means refers to the elegant rendering of the translation in the target language (Chinese) from the perspective of the modern literary point of view, but rather from the perspective of the literary discourse used in the pre-Qin Dynasty period 2,000 years ago. So from this, we find that Yan's third point does not apply to ordinary readers, but those who have not only a strong elite sense but also a high aesthetic attainment which cannot be reached by ordinary readers. Also, from a pragmatic point of view, such translation is apparently a failure, for many of Yan's translations or writings cannot be read by ordinary readers today. As is well-known, the difference between the ancient Chinese language and modern Chinese language is so huge that it is as difficult for Chinese students to grasp the essence of ancient Chinese as it is for them to grasp the essence of modern English. Since the ancient Chinese language is dead and it is Greek to most Chinese people, what is the significance of using it as a criterion for the ideal translation of literary works? So it is not surprising that from the reader's point of view, the third point of Yan's criterion is far from being practical or reasonable. Since the criterion has lost its pragmatic function, it cannot be regarded as a success.

Of course, we should admit that Yan Fu was a politically staunch revolutionary who made great contributions to the overthrow of feudal society. He was, however, culturally conservative, which finds particular embodiment in his "ideal" criterion for translation. Although so many Chinese scholars or translators have tried their best to revise or reinterpret Yan's criterion, I would like to offer my own construction of an ideal criterion on the basis of my understanding or even deliberate misreading of Yan's three points. An ideal criterion for literary translation requires the translator to: (1) read closely and have a thorough understanding of the original text by reading between the lines (the deep structure of the linguistic discourse) and even behind the lines (the implied cultural connotation and literary convention and other necessary background knowledge) and by identifying himself with the author or text; (2) create a perfect rendition which is not only fluent but also preserves the original style without imposing the translator's own subjective construction; (3) improve the translated version until it reaches the high level of modern literary discourse of the target language without changing the original style; and (4) convey in the translation the original text's cultural connotation beyond the mere structural or linguistic level. That is, a translator should first of all identify himself with the original author or text on the same (linguistic rendering) level before transcending himself to a higher (cultural representation) level. If we can achieve this, we can certainly transcend ourselves to the level of translating literature in a cultural context.

SEEKING EQUIVALENCE ON DIFFERENT LEVELS

Actually, the process of translation is always one of looking for an equivalent with which to render the original meaning in the target language. In speaking of equivalence in such a process, one will immediately think of finding the absolute corresponding equivalent word between two languages. But that will not do. Wang Zuoliang sums up on the basis of his own translation practice that in translating literature, one should emphasize these three points: (1) translate the concept and convey the complete feeling of the original rather than just one word; (2) appeal to style, with different genres rendered differently; and (3) pay more attention to the reader.[9] That is, greater importance should be attached to cultural equivalence than to any other aspects. Obviously, equivalence can be achieved, but not always on the same level. Taking English–Chinese translation, for example, we can divide such equivalence into at least four levels: (1) the equivalence on the verbal level, that is, word-for-word translation which usually takes place in rendering a single sentence; (2) the equivalence on the sentence level, without totally breaking up the complete sentence; (3) the equivalence on the passage level, without adding more to the passage; and (4) the equivalence on the textual or even cultural level, that is, rearranging the structure of the text without changing the basic meaning or content of the original text. If we say that the first three kinds of equivalence are linguistically oriented and hence the basic equivalence a translation should achieve, the last one obviously appeals to a sort of cultural equivalence. The first three kinds of equivalence are associated with the surface structure in rendering the original meaning in the target language, while the fourth one is more subtle and more difficult to grasp. To find equivalence on the verbal level is not difficult at all if the translator has some knowledge of the original text and is good at choosing the most appropriate words in a dictionary to convey the original meaning. If we can say a translated sentence is faithful, it means that it finds equivalence on the sentence level. Even to find equivalence on the passage level is just to readjust the order of the sentence structure in the original text or reconstruct some new sentences within one passage. The fourth kind of equivalence is most difficult to achieve and thus most debatable, because it is actually a sort of cultural translation rather than just literal/liberal translation on any of the first three levels. Here, I would like to show an example of a classical Chinese literary text which has been translated by a Western sinologist into perfect modern literary English. The text is Tao Yuanming's "Tao Hua Yuan: shi bing ji" ("The Peach Blossom Spring: Poem and Its Preface"). The following is the full text of the English translation done by James Hightower:

> During the T'ai-yuan period of the Chin dynasty a fisherman of Wuling once rowed upstream, unmindful of the distance he had gone, when he suddenly came to a grove of peach trees in bloom. For several hundred paces on both banks of the stream there was no other kind of tree. The wild flowers growing under them were fresh and lovely, and fallen petals covered the ground—it made a great impression on the fisherman. He went on for a way with the idea of finding out how far the grove extended. It came to an end at the foot of a mountain whence issued the spring that supplied the streams. There was a small opening in the mountain and it seemed as though light was coming through it. The fisherman left his boat and entered the cave, which at first was extremely narrow, barely admitting his body; after a few dozen steps it suddenly opened out onto a broad and level plain where well-built houses were surrounded by rich fields and pretty ponds. Mulberry, bamboo and other trees and plants grew there, and criss-cross paths skirted the fields. The sounds of cocks crowing and dogs barking could be heard from one courtyard to the next. Men and women were coming and going about their work in the fields. The clothes they wore were like those of ordinary people. Old men and boys were carefree and happy.
>
> When they caught sight of the fisherman, they asked in surprise how he had got there. The fisherman told the whole story, and was invited to go to their house, where he was served wine while they killed a chicken for a feast. When the other villagers heard about the fisherman's arrival they all came to pay him a visit. They told him that their ancestors had fled the disorders of Ch'in times and,

having taken refuge here with wives and children and neighbors, had never ventured out again; consequently they had lost all contact with the outside world. They asked what the present ruling dynasty was, for they had never heard of the Han, let alone the Wei and the Chin. They sighed unhappily as the fisherman enumerated the dynasties one by one and recounted the vicissitudes of each. The visitors all asked him to come to their houses in turn, and at every house he had wine and food. He stayed several days. As he was about to go away, the people said, "There's no need to mention our existence to outsiders."

After the fisherman had gone out and recovered his boat, he carefully marked the route. On reaching the city, he reported what he had found to the magistrate, who at once sent a man to follow him back to the place. They proceeded according to the marks he had made, but went astray and were unable to find the cave again.

A high-minded gentleman of Nan-yang named Liu Tzu-chi heard the story and happily made preparations to go there, but before he could leave he fell sick and died. Since then there has been no one interested in trying to find such a place.[10]

Obviously, the translated version is very well done according to the first two points of Yan's criterion. Also, it has helped to debunk the myth that classical Chinese literature, especially classical Chinese poetry, is untranslatable. Although the original text is much shorter and consists of only one paragraph due to the conciseness of ancient Chinese, the English version divides it into four paragraphs, with each clearly identified. The original text is a poetic narration which serves as the preface to the poem "The Peach Blossom Spring", whereas the translated version reads more like an autonomous story, or a sort of national allegory which could be read and interpreted in an allegorical way and which has actually produced some new significance. According to my paradigm, it has only achieved equivalence on the fourth level—that of culture—for English-speaking readers have no difficulty in understanding the general idea of the original text. And it is even easier for the Chinese students of English who do not have a solid foundation in ancient Chinese to understand the text. To this extent, it is a successful translation, for it is both faithful (on the textual level) to the original text and expressive in its rendition in the target language although some minor mistakes have been made in conveying the subtle meaning of the original text. There are, however, still some problems in style, which actually proves that classical Chinese literature is untranslatable with respect to preserving the original style as well as the beauty in sound. The major problem with the translation lies in its changing of the original poetic style into that of prose, thus losing the conciseness of ancient Chinese and its poetic beauty. From the cultural point of view, in reading the English version, the reader who has some knowledge of Freudian psychoanalysis will immediately recognize the psychoanalytic element—the return to the womb—but in reading the original Chinese text, the reader hardly has such a feeling. In this way, we cannot but realize that in Chinese–English translation, it is extremely difficult or even impossible to achieve absolute equivalence, otherwise the translated version will not read like English. Thus, to English-speaking scholars, it is only possible for them to make cultural criticisms rather than aesthetic or formalistic criticisms of "The Peach Blossom Spring".

A TENTATIVE CONCLUSION: DECONSTRUCTING THE BINARY OPPOSITION

Judging from the above example, from the perspective of Chinese–Western comparative culture, we could infer that classical Chinese literature is both translatable and untranslatable to different extents. And such binary opposition as that between the translatability and intranslatability of classical Chinese literature is thus deconstructed. On the level of words, sentences, passages and even text and to the extent of content and basic meaning, classical Chinese literature is translatable, but as it (especially classical Chinese poetry) is characterized by its polysemy, symbolism and frequent use of artistic images and allusions which are themselves rather subtle and ambiguous even to native Chinese speakers, it is untranslatable in this respect, or the translated version is bound to lose something, especially its beauty in form and in sound, if it is translated into English just like what Hightower has done. In this way, absolute equivalence can never be reached although relative equivalence could be reached on different levels depending on the cultural capacity, aesthetic attainment and rendering skills of the translator. We can only approach such equivalence but cannot achieve it completely. Perhaps that is due to the huge difference in culture and literary convention. In this aspect, the present chapter is just an attempt to narrow such a cultural gap and approach the truth.

CHAPTER 7

Translating Theory: Toward a Reconstruction of Chinese Critical Discourse

We have all realized that ours is an age of globalization in which the boundary between nations, cultures, religious beliefs and even academic disciplines has become more and more obscured. The spread of theory is usually realized through the intermediary of translation, which actually functions as one of the major means of cultural communication. As Schulte and Biguenet suggest, "Communication can take place on several levels: the communication through the artistic creation, the communication through the reading and interpretation of texts, and the communication of texts from one language to another by transforming them through the act of translation. At all times, translation involves an act of transformation."[1] Since translation as discussed in the present chapter involves mostly that of culture and literature, I think it is necessary to redefine the concept of translation in its traditional sense, especially in the Chinese–Western cultural and literary context. Obviously, in the Chinese–Western cultural and theoretical exchange, translation also functions as an inevitable means of cultural interpretation rather than mere linguistic rendition. Various critical theories, academic thoughts and cultural trends have travelled from the West to the East, which has, through the intermediary of translation or mistranslation and interpretation or misinterpretation, produced some metamorphosed versions in the Oriental context. So I will first of all describe the new role translation may well play in the age of globalization as a response to the various pessimistic views about the function of translation in the future, and then I will try to distinguish between the reconstruction of

Chinese critical discourse and the so-called "decolonization" of Chinese culture in an attempt to defend the legitimacy of translating theory in its postcolonial and cultural sense.

THE FUNCTION OF TRANSLATION IN THE AGE OF GLOBALIZATION REVISITED

Obviously, in the age of globalization, the traditional concept of time and space has been largely condensed, with information spreading swiftly beyond one's expectation. Our present world is thereby regarded as a vast "global village" in which people from different countries with different cultural backgrounds and even from different continents can easily communicate with each other by various means. Apparently, the most frequently used means is *language*, or more exactly, the English language, which has now been recognized as the most popular international working language, at least in cultural and academic circles. Since translation is primarily a technique of rendering the meaning from one language into another, it serves as a major means by which information is exchanged and interpersonal communication is carried out. But that is only the traditional function of translation in its narrow sense, or linguistic sense. In its broad sense, or its postcolonial and cultural sense, translation also functions as a major means of cultural interpretation or representation. It is the so-called "cultural translation" as described by Homi Bhabha[2] in its postcolonial sense that I will discuss here. How an ideal and most relevant translation is produced has also been heatedly discussed ever since translation came into being. In the Chinese context, Yan Fu's notorious criterion for translation of *xin* (faithfulness), *da* expressiveness) and *ya* (elegance) did play an important role in promoting Chinese political and cultural modernity although it is not largely discussed in the international context. It is true that every translator affirms that he/she is most faithful to the original text and thus understands the original text correctly while doing the translation. But who will be the judge of such translations? Translation scholars or translation theorists as well as the broad reading public, of course. But almost all the scholars or theorists dealing with translation studies usually fail to convince their critics, for there is no such thing as the translated version being exactly faithful to the original text since in the process of representing the same cultural content in another language, something has to be more or less lost both in content and in form. Even the same person cannot precisely repeat the speeches that he has just made, let alone other people expressing them in another language. We are faced with these questions: Can we find a solution to this problem? Or will the authenticity of culture remain intact when it is translated?

Let us start with a critical reflection on the linguistic approach to translation. In this respect, translation scholars or theorists from one generation to another have tried hard to find such a solution. Eugene Nida, who is frequently quoted and discussed in the Chinese context, once offered his concept of "dynamic equivalence" in which the translator "aims at complete naturalness of expression, and tries to relate the receptor to modes of behavior relevant within the context of his own culture".[3] Here, in Nida's view, since translation already touches upon the question of culture, complete equivalence is impossible and unnecessary due to the difference between cultures. So he tries to find a relatively relevant way to represent the original meaning expressed in the source language by putting forward this "dynamic equivalence" as he understands the dynamic function of the translator. This is, of course, by no means a breakthrough in translation studies as he puts forward this strategy from his traditional linguistic perspective, but it may be a tentative solution starting from the linguistic angle. Although Nida's theoretical construction highlights the (dynamic or subjective) function of the translator, we easily find that his perspective is based on the level of linguistics, or the interlinguistic rather than intercultural observation of translation.

Since Nida is chiefly a linguist, or a scholar of translation studies from the linguistic perspective, his theoretic concept has been questioned and even bypassed by scholars of translation studies of the later generation, both in the West and even in China. Jacques Derrida, as a deconstructive theorist or theoretic translator in a broad cultural sense, has made much effort to approach a sort of "relevant" translation by transcending the old conventions. To Derrida, although a completely "relevant" translation is impossible, a relatively "relevant" translation could be achieved if the translator tries his best to do so. Here, it is the process itself rather than its effect that is of significance. To my mind, Derrida's attempt has actually deconstructed a sort of myth that the original meaning could be repeated, and the same is true of cultural authenticity. If it could be done, what does translation mean after all? According to the traditional definition of translation, the basic meaning of translation is to "change from one language into another", or more broadly, to "change from one form into another". Although this "change" largely appeals to form rather than content, the translator who practises this change cannot adhere exactly to the original text even if he/she wants to. That is why we have such a saying that the "translator is equivalent to a traitor". Fortunately, the postmodernist/poststructuralist doctrine has liberated translators from the theoretic and cultural impasse highlighting their own interpretive subjectivity. Any sense of centre or finality of truth or authenticity has been deconstructed in the process of a deconstructive reading and interpretation. Apparently, in Derrida's theoretical concept, we have already seen a shift of focus in (relevant) translation from "purely" linguistic rendition to dynamic and cultural interpretation and representation. In this sense, we should say that Derrida himself is more a great theoretic and cultural interpreter (translator) than a translator in its traditional sense. And the role played by the translator is more of a "revisionist" rather than a "traitor", for the former usually "revises" the original text in the target language by adhering to it in the source language, but the latter deliberately moves away from the original text in an attempt to "create" something new. Derrida obviously likes the word, but to him, the word appears as "Word" rather than its literal meaning.

Undoubtedly, different scholars or translators explore the issue of relevant translation from their own angles. My perspective is certainly that of culture, although I always hold that literal translation in certain contexts is absolutely essential to represent the very meaning of the original text in a comparatively faithful way, especially in the translation of scientific documents. In literary translation, however, it is of utmost importance to represent the very subtle meaning between the lines and even behind the lines. Literary works usually imply very subtle cultural and aesthetic connotations that are untranslatable if the translator merely adheres to the superficial fidelity on the linguistic level. Sometimes, as agreed upon among all literary translators, it is necessary to add some interpretations to the original text so that the reader will be able to understand the translated text more easily. In this sense, literary translation is more like cultural interpretation and aesthetic representation than mere linguistic rendition. Thus, equivalence on the verbal level or sentence level is sometimes impossible and unnecessary, for according to this standard, Lin Shu—one of the pioneering figures in China's literary translation—cannot even be seen as a translator, although the important role he played in the process of advancing China's cultural modernity and the history of modern (translated) Chinese literature is generally recognized.

Frankly speaking, as for the criterion of the so-called "cultural authenticity," modern Chinese literature is nothing but a "translated literature", for largely through the translation of Western literary works and cultural and academic trends, Chinese literature has gradually formed a new tradition, or a sort of modern Chinese literary canon, which is both different from its Western counterpart as well as from its established tradition, and which is able to engage in dialogue with both classical Chinese literature as well as with Western literature. In this respect, Lin Shu has translated, with the help of some young Chinese scholars who understand Western languages, a lot of literary works into Chinese. His unique contributions cannot be neglected, for many of his contemporary fellow writers were influenced more by his (translated) texts of Western literary works than directly by the original authors. Although Lin almost did not do any theoretical translation, his literary translation practice has undoubtedly offered lots of exemplary texts for translation theorists and scholars of the later generation to discuss and interpret from a cultural perspective.[4] Thus, to an excellent literary translator, to be faithful in spirit and style is much more difficult than to be faithful merely in words and sentences; it is a sort of fidelity on the highest and most ideal level. Hence, I would like to re-emphasize that it is necessary to redefine translation in a new context since its old definition has been largely challenged and debated for many years, for along with the deepening of cultural studies, more and more scholars have realized that translation has much to do with culture, and cultural connotations cannot be rendered merely on the linguistic level. Therefore, it is possible to do translation studies in the broader context of cultural studies as translation touches on at least two or more different cultures. It should not be viewed as just a matter of "pure" literal rendition of the meaning of the original (source) language in another (target) language.

Although Derrida clearly realizes that it is almost impossible to achieve an absolutely relevant translation, it is worth trying to approach such an ideal. To him, the reason why Shylock in Shakespeare's *The Merchant of Venice* fails in court is largely because he could not get the "exactly one pound" of flesh, no more and no less, from Antonio. Or in Terry Eagleton's words, "What individuals share most vitally in common is the body: it is by virtue of our bodies that we belong to each other, and no cultural or linguistic community which is not somehow founded upon this fact is likely to survive. For the texts in which Shylock trusts—the Old Testament—the body is not in the first place a physical object but a form of relationship, a principle of unity with others."[5] Therefore, in the rendition of language, meaning cannot "faithfully" repeat itself once you have expressed it in a language. What a translator can achieve is just a comparatively "good" translation or relatively "faithful" interpretation, which appears as relevant as possible and as faithful as possible to the original text, for every translator is first of all a human who has his own dynamic understanding, creative reception and constructive representation of the original text. So his interpretation represents to a large extent his own subjectivity and dynamic reception of the original text, in the process of which some revision rather than deliberate "betrayal" is unavoidable. That is perhaps the ideal "relevant" translation to my understanding.

Then, what will translation be like in the present age of globalization, which appears as a ghost-like spectre haunting our memories every now and then and influencing our cultural and intellectual life as well as our academic research? Obviously, globalization is not something created by scholars, but rather an objective phenomenon in our daily life. If we recognize that economic globalization started with the discovery of the Americas in 1492 by Columbus, then cultural globalization would have started even earlier. Under the impact of globalization, the cultural and literary market has been shrinking. The humanities and social sciences are severely challenged by the overload of knowledge and the swift exchange of information. On the other hand, the function of the English language is much more obvious: All scientific papers should be published in English if their authors intend to have them recognized by their international colleagues, and people from different parts of the world usually communicate in English rather than in their own languages if they do not depend upon the help of interpreters. In this way, English is playing an increasingly important role in such a global information society. We can easily get access to most of the information on the Internet by means of English. If we get access to information, we can easily survive in the present era, and if we have a good command of English, we can get even more information. If we still believe that knowledge is strength, then in the age of globalization, information is power. And the old slogan, "Knowledge is strength", put forward by

Francis Bacon should be changed to the present "Knowledge is riches". Thus, translation is all the more necessary in such an age of globalization, although more and more people are learning to communicate directly in English. But in the present era of globalization, it is the translation of native languages into English, or sometimes even the translation of (postcolonial) "English(es)" into the (Imperial) standard English rather than vice versa. Therefore, in the age of globalization, the demand for translators is even higher, and competent translators with comprehensive and profound knowledge are badly needed although more and more people are learning to use the English language as the major means of their communication.

It is true that economic globalization has given rise to cultural globalization in which Western, or particularly American, culture is imposing its values upon Third World culture. So some non-English-speaking people are very much worried about the possible "colonization" of their cultures and languages. What then is the function of translation in the age of globalization since cultures are becoming more and more homogenized? First of all, we should recognize that the impact of globalization is embodied at two poles: its effect travels from the West to the East and, at the same time, from the East to the West. Dialectically speaking, globalization has created linkages between different social and cultural phenomena, such as identities, social relationships and even institutions, and these linkages must be placed within a specific historical context. In the age of globalization, communication between different societies, cultures and nations is taking place more and more frequently. But how can such communication be carried out more effectively? Undoubtedly by means of information exchanges in which language— or more specifically, the English language—plays the most important role. Just as Schulte and Biguenet pertinently point out, "The interaction with the words of the foreign language expands one's native language. To produce equivalencies for certain metaphors in the source language, the translator may have to find words in English that are normally not part of general usage. Thus writers who are involved in translating enrich their own language."[6] The birth of the new Chinese literary language during the May 4th period was largely due to such English–Chinese translation. From this point of view, I think that translation is ever more inevitable, functioning not only as a major means of daily communication, but also as a major means of cultural exchange and political strategy. It has gone far beyond the superficial level of linguistic aspects, so the research on translation should attach more importance to the cultural aspects of translation.

I am of the opinion that although current cultural studies in the English-speaking world has exerted a strong influence on, or even severely challenged, literary studies, it should not necessarily influence translation studies as translation is first of all an issue of culture, hence translation studies forms part of cultural studies. Even in the "global village" today, cultural communication and exchange should still be attained by means of translation. So I hold that in the age of globalization, however marginalized literature and other cultural forms might be, translation will not disappear, but rather, it will still occupy a vital place in our cultural and intellectual life as well as in our daily communication. No matter how effective or powerful the translation machine may be, it cannot take the place of human beings, for it is human beings who are able to master the nuances of different cultures and theories and represent them in a comparatively relevant way. And it is human beings who are able to judge whether the translation is relevant or not. If we apply this principle to literary and cultural translation, it will prove even more effective.

TRANSLATING THEORY: DECOLONIZING CHINESE CULTURE?

It is true that the advent of modernity in China is largely a direct consequence of cultural translation, both of Western literary works as well as various cultural trends and academic thoughts. In this respect, apart from Yan Fu, who has already been largely discussed elsewhere, Lin Shu, Kang Youwei and Liang Qichao have also played pioneering roles in helping to bring Western modernity into the Chinese context by means of translation. Lu Xun, Hu Shi, Guo Moruo and many other pioneering figures of modern Chinese literature and Chinese cultural modernity also enthusiastically called for more and more academic theories and cultural trends to be translated from foreign countries, especially from the West. The famous catch-phrase put forward by Lu Xun at the time was "grabbism" (*nalai zhuyi*); that is, grab anything useful to the Chinese practice so as to give thorough critiques of traditional Chinese culture. Some of these Chinese writers, such as Guo Moruo and Cao Yu, even tried to identify themselves with their Western masters: Guo called himself "China's Whitman" as his poetic writing was under the direct influence of Walt Whitman, and Cao was known as "China's

Ibsen" as he started his dramatic career by playing the role of Nora, one of Ibsen's major heroines. During the May 4th period, translating literature and theory meant the modernizing and democratizing of China politically and culturally. Democracy and science—labelled Mr. De and Mr. Sai respectively—did play important roles in China's process of political democratization and cultural modernization, which has undoubtedly paved the way for the later advent of globalization in the late twentieth century. Thus, we should say that translation of literature and theory at the time was largely done at the level of culture, or more exactly, at the level of the pragmatic function of these literary works and theories in China's modernity project.[7] As a result, many theoretical doctrines and literary works were not even translated from their original languages, but from either English or Japanese, let alone being faithful to the original works.[8] But we should recognize that the function of translation at the time was inadequately highlighted as a powerful instrument of revolution and democratization. Thus, the translation of theory has indeed played a significant role in China's advances in modernity and new literary and critical discourse which is somewhat "colonized" from a conservative point of view but gradually getting closer to the outside world from an international point of view. The May 4th Movement from 1919 to 1949 that marked the beginning of new Chinese literature and culture, usually called "modern Chinese literature", even speeded up the process of modernization in the Chinese context. During that period of time, translation was really flourishing, with all the prevalent Western cultural trends and theories translated into Chinese; such Western masters as Schopenhauer, Bergson, Nietzsche and Freud were frequently discussed in Chinese intellectuals' salons as well as in their books and influenced their intellectual lives and academic research. All three major Western literary currents—romanticism, realism and modernism—came onto the literary scene chronologically through translation, which in turn produced some different versions of "Chinese characteristics", and which indeed paved the way for the later, more extensive, translation of postmodern and postcolonial theories and literary works in the 1990s.

Of all the translators in the turn of the last century, and later in the May 4th period, Lin Shu's contributions were the most conspicuous and even unprecedented. From today's linguistic point of view, although Lin Shu's translation cannot be regarded as being "relevant" on the linguistic level since his "translation" was largely done with the help of someone else who understood a Western language, his "translation" on the cultural and theoretical level was successful if we evaluate it from a historical and cultural point of view. Through his dynamic translation and even creative interpretation, all the Western literary works and academic thoughts produced new significance in the Chinese context. By and by, these translated "texts" have become part of Chinese literary culture, influencing writers and scholars from one generation to the next. Since his translated works are characterized by elegance and readability and even attractiveness, they have been largely regarded as a part of modern Chinese literature. Obviously, translated literature in China is such a significant and essential part of modern Chinese literature that many of today's writers would admit that they are influenced by Western (translated) literature rather than by classical Chinese literature. And many of today's scholars and critics would admit that they are inspired by their Western masters' (translated) works rather than by their Chinese ancestors. In this sense, we should say that the translation of theory has played an even more important role in either "colonizing" Chinese literary discourse or helping to form a new "translated" literary or critical discourse.

The May 4th period has long become part of history although its historical significance is still controversial. We live in an age of globalization, in which we can communicate more easily in such a vast "global village" with the floating of so much information. An information society endows us with a vast cyberspace in which we can exchange views and information more easily and more directly if we have a good grasp of English. Translation in its traditional sense as well as its studies in China, although more or less "marginalized" for a long period as a sub-discipline under foreign linguistics and applied linguistics, is still developing in full swing.[9] After the Cultural Revolution, China opened itself more widely to the outside world and practised economic reform, and more and more Western cultural trends, literary works and critical theories are flooding into the country. No sooner had we caught up with the trend of modernism than we encountered postmodernism. It was not long before modernity became an old-fashioned cultural concept or theoretical discourse although it has been associated with postmodernity in today's context of globalization. It has been more or less replaced by other discourses—postmodernity and globalization— although some people think that even in the age of globalization, modernity is still an incomplete concept, with postmodernity being a part of it.[10] With various postmodern theories as effective interpretive instruments, we can analyze and interpret various cultural phenomena in the context of globalization. Obviously, such "translation" or mistranslation and interpretation in the sense of culture and critical theory will more or less "colonize" or "hybridize" Chinese critical discourse, which is characterized by its weak or non-existent voice in international theoretical debate. The Chinese cultural identity has thus been obscured under the impact of globalization. But just as Gayatri Spivak has relevantly pointed out, "there is often a certain loss of style in the descent or shift from the high culture of nationalism within territorial Imperialism to that search for 'national identity' that confuses religion, culture, and ideology in the newly independent nation".[11] As a successful postcolonial intellectual moving from the "periphery" to the centre and finally becoming one of the "world's foremost contemporary theorists",[12] Spivak started her academic career by translating theory, or more specifically, translating and interpreting Jacques Derrida's deconstructive critical theory, which largely influenced her own critical theory and even helped to form her own critical discourse characterized by postcoloniality and Third World criticism. Now we cannot but admit that Spivak is a very influential postcolonial critic with her own unique voice and theoretical discourse and even her own writing style. The influences of Marx, Nietzsche, Derrida and Paul de Man have been assimilated and, in turn, have helped to form her own postcolonial style and critical discourse. Actually, it is not Spivak who is "colonized" by others, but Spivak who is "colonizing" or influencing others. The same is true of Homi Bhabha, whose postcolonial criticism is somewhat characterized by his appeal to a sort of "cultural translation", and who has recently started his strategy of "minoritization" as opposed to the "grand" narrative of globalization.[13]

Since China is a large country with a 5,000-year-long history and splendid cultural heritage and rich literary tradition, it has never been totally "colonized" before, nor will it be "colonized" in the future even if we introduce as many Western theoretical works as possible through translation. It goes without saying that we should not worry about the "colonizing" of Chinese culture. On the contrary, many sinologists, in their teachings and studies of Chinese culture, have been "sinicized" due to their esteem and respect for China and its culture and literature, and the successful production of some Chinese films has actually helped Western audiences to understand Chinese culture despite the fact that the films have to be more or less "Orientalized" by the Western means of translation or aesthetic representation or sometimes even coincide with the Western audiences' "horizon of expectation".[14] In international communication and cultural exchange, we cannot say that we can preserve every aspect of our culture, especially in translating our culture into another language. We might well lose something if we want our foreign audience to understand the translation. The same is true of Lin Shu's translation of Western literary works into Chinese, which has indeed lost a lot of things but still preserves the cultural spirit of the Western literary works. So to my mind, such a "loss" of our national and cultural identity is no doubt a necessary step toward a conscious construction and even reconstruction of Chinese critical discourse. Thus, truly equitable theoretical dialogue between Chinese and Western literary and cultural scholarship will take place in the present age of globalization.

RECONSTRUCTING CHINESE CRITICAL DISCOURSE BY MEANS OF TRANSLATION

As mentioned previously, in the age of globalization, the spread of theory is not just always from the West to the East, or from the centre to the periphery; sometimes, it occurs from the periphery to the centre, functioning both at the centre and periphery and finally deconstructing the monolithic Imperial centre. For the advent of globalization has broken down the demarcation between nations and countries, and between the centre and the periphery, with transnational corporations functioning as an "empire" everywhere. In this way, globalization does not always appear as a "ghost-like" spectre troubling our lives and work and haunting our memories every now and then. It has also benefited people who want to get out of the isolated domain, enabling them to communicate more effectively in such a "global village". In academic research, it stimulates scholars to internationalize and even globalize their research results in a more effective way. And it has therefore enabled us Chinese scholars to communicate more easily with the international scholarship on any theoretical and academic topics, including translation studies.[15] But unfortunately, for a long period of time, Chinese scholars of translation studies had little or even no voice in international theoretical debates on the issues of translation despite the fact that Chinese translators have indeed done a lot of translation in pushing China to the state of modernity, both politically and culturally. In the past few decades since China opened up to the outside world and carried out economic reform, this unfavourable situation has been changed somewhat, with more and more articles appearing in international journals in English or French and more and more scholars speaking with a stronger and more forceful voice in international translation studies circles.[16] How should we realize our goal of internationalizing and even globalizing China's translation studies when we are confronted with a much more powerful Western empire that has an omnipresent language as well as penetrating critical discourse? That is what I will highlight with our own practical strategy.

Obviously, as I have already mentioned, the spread of theory is not always from the centre to the periphery; it sometimes spreads from the periphery to the centre and functions both at the centre as well as the periphery. This finds particular embodiment in the spread of Bakhtin's theory, from Russia (cultural periphery at the time) to the West (centre) and back to Russia (periphery), and finally over the world. As one of the major thinkers of the twentieth century, Mikhail Bakhtin's writings cover "linguistics, psychoanalysis, theology, social theory, historical poetics, axiology, and philosophy of the person".[17] His works are so widely ranged that they cover almost all the major disciplines in the humanities and human thinking in the twentieth century. His research has also found its way into many theoretical approaches, including feminism, postmodernism, cultural studies, and even the emerging field of ecocriticism. It was in the very isolated atmosphere in the former Soviet Union that Bakhtin wrote all his important works without referring to the then prevalent Western critical theories. But his theories, characterized by dialogism, have actually engaged in dialogue with both structuralist and poststructuralist doctrines and illuminated them to such an extent that Bakhtin studies was once all the rage in the West, and even in China for some time. And Bakhtin's works have been translated and retranslated by one critical school after another, in the process of which a new "Bakhtin" has been "constructed" in different cultural contexts. Although Bakhtin probably could not have anticipated such wide expropriation of his ideas, they have indeed been received favourably in various theoretical fields and "discovered" or "translated" and "rediscovered" or "retranslated" by both structuralists and poststructuralists. This phenomenon first appeared in the West in the mid-1970s when Bakhtin's works were translated into Western languages. But translating Bakhtin's works finally culminated in China with *Bahejin quanji* (Collected Works of Bakhtin) published in Chinese in seven volumes in 1998.[18] Obviously, the translation of theory has enabled Bakhtin's doctrine to function both in the centre (West) and periphery (Russia and China), bridging the gap between the centre and the periphery and finally obscuring this artificial demarcation. The Bakhtin phenomenon has illuminated us Chinese scholars in our theoretical dialogue with both our Western and international colleagues.

As open-minded scholars engaged in international academic and theoretical communication, how should we be inspired by the spread and translation of Bakhtin's theory? First of all, we should not be afraid of the spread and translation of Western theory into China, for the globalization of culture is not necessarily the same as that of the economy. Cultural plurality and diversity always exist in spite of the severe challenge of economic globalization. It has brought about both cultural homogenization as well as cultural diversity, with the latter more evident in today's context. Overwhelming historical evidence has proved that an economically powerful Imperial empire cannot necessarily produce aesthetically elegant works of art, whereas on the contrary, it is those less developed or even underdeveloped countries where the economic strength is comparatively weak and the cultural soil of modernity is rather thin which produce excellent artistic works. This was demonstrated in the field of literary creation, in the rise of Russian realistic novels and their critical theories in the late nineteenth century and the "booming" of Latin American "magic realist" novels. In literary theory and criticism, the critical and creative reception of postmodernism in China and the appearance of the metamorphosed versions of a sort of "Chinese postmodernity" will further prove this.[19] The introduction and translation of Western theories into Chinese today does not mean writing off our own culture and critical discourse, but vice versa. That is, we must at least get a clear idea of the state of the art of how our Western colleagues are researching critical theory before we can realize our second purpose; that is to say, finding topics of common interest on which we can have equitable dialogue, and during which our own theoretical and critical discourse is constructed or reconstructed. In this way, our voice in the international forum will be really strong and forceful.

At the moment, it is impossible for all the people from other parts of the world to listen to us in Chinese, partly because this language is too difficult to master and partly because at present, China's economy is not strong enough as to be able to support all the foreigners in their study of China's language and culture.[20] Even if our Western colleagues master the Chinese language, it is still difficult for them to understand the nuances of Chinese culture and the subtlety of the Chinese aesthetic spirit. So what we can do for the time being in communicating with the international community is to use the English language, by means of which we can introduce our excellent cultural products and theoretical works to the world. As for the critical and theoretical discourse borrowed from the West, we have to use them in communicating with our Western colleagues if we want to convince them with our own theoretical constructions. But even so, these "borrowed" discourses have already been "hybridized" and mixed with indigenous Chinese critical and theoretical discourses when we are using them. Including the Chinese critical practice starting from Chinese literary creation, these discourses have not only been "metamorphosed" but have also produced new significance that will, in turn, inspire and influence our Western colleagues. This is just the spread of theory in the other direction.

From the perspective of cultural translation, we should say that Lin Shu's translation or representation of Western literary works in the turn of the last century set a good example for us to follow although we must first of all lay a solid foundation of foreign languages before starting such translation work. But in today's context of globalization, Lin's old-fashioned method cannot function effectively and relevantly as more and more people have mastered the English language and effectively use it in international communication and literary translation. Therefore, cultural aspects will become more and more conspicuous and relevant in our practice of translation if we really want to "globalize" our Chinese culture, literature and literary theory.

CHAPTER 8

Translation as Cultural "Decolonization"

As far as the meaning of translation in today's context of globalization is concerned, there has already been a variety of descriptions or definitions of this indeterminate phenomenon or practice, either from the linguistic perspective or from the literary perspective, or even from the cross-cultural perspective as translation studies has in recent years been more and more closely linked to cultural studies. Although I myself have redefined translation by relating it to currently prevailing cultural studies on other occasions, I would like to confirm once again that translation, in the final analysis, is a matter of culture, especially in speaking of translation as literary representation and cultural interpretation with regard to its function of cultural communication and interpretation. Anyone doing translation or undertaking translation studies today cannot but encounter the elements of culture. To translate a literary work of rich cultural connotation means to represent and even interpret the subtle and rich cultural content and aesthetic spirit inherent in the literary work in another language. But how does culture manipulate the practice of translation? And how does translation "colonize" or "decolonize" a certain culture if it undertakes this task? This is what the present chapter will deal with in a critical and theoretical way, especially with regard to the development of modern Chinese culture and the historical development of modern Chinese literature, in the process of which translated literature has played an irreplaceable and inseparable part in the formation of Chinese cultural and literary modernity.

TRANSLATION AS A DYNAMIC CULTURAL REPRESENTATION

It is true that translation has long been in existence both in China and the West when people started to communicate with each other. Literary translation has played an even more important part in enabling people of different countries or nations or cultural backgrounds and speaking different languages to read and appreciate excellent literary works in other languages or cultural traditions. Without the intermediary of translation, we could never expect to read the original Homeric epics in Greek, nor could most of the Western readers appreciate the beauty of the original Chinese poetry of the Tang and Song Dynasties. Thus, translation actually bridges different nations, crossing cultural and linguistic boundaries. A good translation will bring excellent cultural products from one cultural tradition to another, thereby realizing the "spread of literature" and enriching literary creation in that nation, while a bad translation will undoubtedly degrade the originally good literary works. But how do we reach the level of a good or relevant translation since the criterion of translation is always indeterminate? Obviously, as is proved by much evidence, there is no such thing as a "purely" good or relevant translation as long as the translation is done by human beings and the criterion is formulated by human beings as well, for a translator is not a machine, but a human being with his/her own dynamic understanding—and sometimes creative reception—of the original text he/she comes across. In doing the translation, his/her own understanding or even misunderstanding of the original text might well influence his/her representation or misrepresentation of it in the target language. And his/her cultural and linguistic competence will also decide whether he/she can provide a translated version that is closer to the original text both in linguistic form and in cultural and aesthetic spirit.

Although it is almost impossible to reach the level of absolutely correct or "relevant" translation, it is still worth exploring this criterion. Jacques Derrida, who is always suspicious of any type of finality of truth in deconstructing all the logocentric doctrines or concepts in Western culture and metaphysics, could not but give his tentative description of what a relevant translation is like. Although Derrida, as a deconstructionist in decentralizing any assumed cultural or linguistic "centre", clearly realizes that it is almost impossible to achieve a really relevant translation, he feels it is worth trying to approach such an ideal as what all the postmodernist theorists appeal to is the process rather than the result itself. His own deconstructive reading has actually blurred the line between literature and philosophy, and anticipated a sort of "end" of philosophy (in its traditional sense). According to the deconstructive doctrine, therefore, you may only approach the truth, but can never grasp the truth. Thus, the translation of culture and theory is nothing but a cycle of interpretation with the finality of truth (original meaning) always remaining absent. The same is true of the translation and interpretation of a literary text as literary connotation is both rich and inclusive, open to different understandings and even different interpretations. Translation is actually an act of dialogic practice; that is, the translator is always having dialogues with both the author and the text, and sometimes even with the reader, thus the translated "meaning" or significance is produced in the process of such dialogic practice. In this way, pursuing a relevant translation is just like searching for the Holy Grail, in which the perfect final result will never be achieved.

Obviously, since literary works are composed of arbitrary aesthetic signs which are rather indeterminate, it is almost impossible to "faithfully" represent the subtle cultural nuances of a certain work of art in the target language. Especially in cross-cultural translation, like English–Chinese translation or vice versa, this irrelevant translation process will manifest itself all the more clearly. It is true that translation theorists or scholars both in China and the West have made much effort to find an efficient way to faithfully render the linguistic meaning of the source language in the target language without changing the original meaning. But their efforts have so far proven unsuccessful. Yan Fu, a pioneering Chinese translation theorist as well as a practitioner in the exploration of such a criterion whose notorious but controversial criterion for a good literary translation has been debated over ever since it was put forward, once tried to rank his three criteria as *xin* (faithfulness), *da* (expressiveness) and *ya* (elegance). In his hierarchy of criteria, faithfulness always comes first, but as for the extent of faithfulness, he did not elaborate clearly, nor has his own translation practice proved effective. In this way, his criterion, partly due to the lack of theoretical elaboration, and more importantly due to the lack of emphasis on cultural elements, has not totally convinced translators although it has actually left much room for further discussion and exploration. That is why today's Chinese translation scholars usually discuss the translation criterion by starting with Yan's three criteria. Frankly speaking, despite the rapid development of translation theory and translation studies in the West, we Chinese translation scholars have made few advances in trying to push forward Chinese translation studies in the context of international dialogue. That is also one of the important reasons why most of the Chinese translation scholars are not able to carry out equitable dialogues with their international counterparts. It is not merely a language problem, but rather theoretical and cultural problems, as all translators have a grasp of at least one foreign language and should be familiar with at least two different cultures.

Eugene Nida, a Western linguist who is largely discussed and quoted in the Chinese context, tries to highlight the translator's dynamic role in rendering text from the source language into the target language. To Nida, since translation touches on the issue of culture, absolute equivalence is impossible and unnecessary due to the minute difference between two or more than two cultures. But the word "receptor" that he uses is still much less dynamic as compared with the word "recipient" used by theorists of the aesthetics of reception. But in order to practise his dynamic strategy, he tries to find a comparatively relevant way to represent the original meaning expressed in the source language by putting forward this "dynamic equivalence" as he understands the dynamic function of the translator. Obviously, his solution has stepped to the fore in the exploration of the dynamic function of culture in the process of translation. Although Nida has indeed emphasized the dynamic function of the translator, we have no difficulty ascertaining that his perspective is based on the level of linguistics, or the interlinguistic rather than intercultural observation of translation. So his strategy cannot be put into effect when doing literary translation.

One may then pose the question: What is literary translation? What is the difference between literary translation and other translation practices? To answer these two questions, I shall first of all describe the former. Literary translation, in my view, should be regarded as the highest form of all translation practices, for it is more closely related to culture than linguistics even though literature is first of all an art of language. As an art, it not only appeals to "faithful" representation, but more to "dynamic" creation or recreation. That is, literary translation could be regarded as an act of creation based on a given original text. And literary work is certainly characterized by a rich cultural connotation and dynamic aesthetic spirit. A literary translator should first of all be an excellent creative writer himself/herself as his/her translation may determine whether or not the literary work can be appreciated by readers of the target language. Sometimes, a successful translation might well play a superb role of revising the established canon, resulting in a sort of canon reformation.[1] So in this sense, the translator is a revisionist rather than a "traitor" as he/she always "revises" the original text based on his/her subjective understanding and dynamic interpretation of it. That is why literary translation has attracted great attention from both comparatists as well as cultural studies scholars in their theoretical debates and exploration, for they both pay particular attention to the function of translation in literary canon formation and reformation.

FROM "COLONIZING" TO "DECOLONIZING": RECONSTRUCTING MODERN CHINESE LITERARY CULTURE

Translation no doubt plays an important role in our cultural and intellectual life, even in today's context of globalization where English is becoming increasingly popular with more and more people in the present world studying and using it both in academic research and in daily communication. If you want to get access to information on the Internet, you had better understand English as most of the information on the Internet is in English. If you want to venture outside of your own country, you should at least know some English if you do not want to isolate yourself from other people. As language is a major means of maintaining national and cultural identity, we will still need the process of translation on many occasions. In speaking of the globalization of literature and culture, we cannot but think of the current tendency of the English language proper, which is also undergoing a sort of "splitting" or metamorphosis from one (standard) form of English into many (indigenous) forms of English as English has become a world language by means of which different national cultures could produce their own literature in English or "English". As Paul Jay illustrates:

> With this awareness it has become increasingly difficult to study British or American literature without situating it, and the culture(s) from which it emerged, in transnational histories linked to globalization. At the same time the remarkable explosion of English literature produced outside Britain and the United States has made it clear that this literature is becoming defined less by nation than by a language, in which authors from a variety of cultural and ethnic backgrounds write. The globalization of English from this point of view is not a theoretical formulation or a political agenda developed by radicals in the humanities to displace the canon. English literature is increasingly postnational... want to argue that we can more effectively reorganize our approach to the study of what we have heretofore treated as national literatures (in our curricula and programs) by emphasizing literature's relation to the historical

progresses of globalization. Such a step involves rejecting the idea that globalization is a fundamentally contemporary event and recognizing that it has a long history.[2]

In fact, globalization is not a contemporary event at all, but rather a process started long before the latter part of the twentieth century. Similarly, along with the process of globalization of culture, the Chinese language has also been undergoing a sort of "splitting" or metamorphosis from one form of Chinese (Mandarin) to many (indigenous) forms of Chinese. That is, we have Mainland Chinese (with numerous local dialects), Cantonese Chinese (spoken both in Guangdong and in Hong Kong), Taiwanese Chinese (with lots of local dialects), Singaporean Chinese, and the Chinese spoken in overseas Chinese communities, etc. Thus, we have two sorts of Chinese literature: literature produced in mainland China, and literature produced elsewhere in the Chinese language.[3] Although domestic intellectuals might well question where we should "locate" our culture in such a context of globalization when different cultures are becoming more and more homogenized, we cannot but realize that the "'locality' of national culture is neither unified nor unitary in relation to itself, nor must it be seen simply as 'other' in relation to what is outside or beyond it".[4] In my view, along with the acceleration of globalization of culture, such a splitting of some of the world's major languages will take place more and more frequently, which may well bring about the pluralistic development of national cultures. Thus, the process of translation will become all the more indispensable.

I also agree with Roland Robertson that globalization is by no means a twentieth-century event, especially with regard to culture. If we acknowledge that economic globalization started with Columbus' discovery of America in 1492, then the globalization of culture started even before that time. In this process, translation has been playing a significant role in accelerating the process of cultural globalization. In order to catch up with the advanced countries both in terms of the economy and culture, people of the underdeveloped countries always take great pains to learn from the advanced countries, in the areas of science and technology as well as the economy, management and culture, in an attempt to import from those advanced countries not only science and technology but also literature and culture. In the history of modern Chinese literature and culture, translation did play a significant role in contributing to China's cultural modernity and reconstructing the literary and critical discourse of modern Chinese literature. Apart from Yan Fu, Kang Youwei, Liang Qichao and Lin Shu also made great contributions to Chinese cultural modernity by enthusiastically calling for the translation of foreign literary and academic works. Their theoretical advocates and practical efforts paved the way for the comprehensive translation of Western cultural trends and literary works into Chinese in the latter part of the twentieth century. It is from these translated literary works that the May 4th writers obtained inspiration for their creative writing. So for those May 4th writers, especially Lu Xun, Guo Moruo and Ba Jin, what influenced their writing most was not necessarily traditional Chinese culture and literature, but rather (translated) foreign literature, especially Western culture and literature. It is therefore not surprising that to some conservative Chinese intellectuals, translation actually played the role of "colonizing" modern Chinese culture and literature, which has obviously departed from the long tradition of classical Chinese culture and literature, as a result of which the first wave of "Westernization" occurred in the first half of the twentieth century, with Chinese literary and critical discourse as well as cultural norms largely becoming Westernized or "colonized".

In the current age of globalization, this "colonizing" trend appears even more conspicuous with more and more people learning to speak and write in English. In such a postindustrial information society, information means power, and information means riches. In order to have their research achievements recognized by the international academic world, scientists have to publish their articles in English in some prestigious international journals. It is true of our humanities and social sciences as well. Therefore, on the other hand, since translation deals at least with two cultures or more, this sort of cultural "colonization", if it exists, is not a one-dimensional phenomenon. Globalization, in homogenizing world culture(s), has also brought about cultural plurality, according to Roland Robertson. The fact that more and more Chinese people are studying English and using it on various occasions means that translation has also changed its traditional role, from converting foreign culture and literature into Chinese to converting Chinese culture and literature into other languages, mostly English. In this way, people of other countries can read and appreciate excellent Chinese literature and cultural products through the intermediary of translation or by means of English. The successful bid to host the 2008 Olympic Games in Beijing is one of the most recent examples, in which the translation from Chinese into English and French indeed played a critical role.[5]

At the moment, it is obviously impossible for all the people from other parts of the world to listen to us in Chinese, partly because this language is too difficult to master and partly because at present, China's economy is not strong enough as to be able to support all the foreigners in their study of the Chinese language and culture. Even if our Western colleagues master the Chinese language, it is still difficult for them to understand the nuances of Chinese culture and the subtlety of the Chinese aesthetic spirit. So what we can do for the time being in more effectively communicating with the international community is to use the English language—the most popular international language—by means of which we can translate and introduce our excellent cultural products to the world. As for the critical and theoretical discourses borrowed from the West, we have to use them in communicating with our Western colleagues if we want to convince them with our own theoretical constructions. But even so, these "borrowed" discourses have already been mixed with indigenous Chinese critical and theoretical discourses when we frequently use them and "localize" them in the Chinese context. Including the Chinese critical practice starting from Chinese literary creation, these discourses have not only been "metamorphosed" and "sinicized" but have also produced new significance that will, in turn, inspire and influence our Western colleagues. Thus, the binary opposition between cultural "colonization" and cultural "decolonization" should be deconstructed since translation could play a dual role in international cultural communication and dialogue.

TOWARD A SORT OF "GLOCALIZATION" OF CULTURAL TRANSLATION

Undoubtedly, we are in the age of globalization, in which one of the characteristic features of cultural representation is the trend of homogenization; that is, influential (hegemonic or First World) cultures are always imposing their cultural values and aesthetic principles on those less influential (Third World) cultures through translation, which is also manifested in literary translation practice. But on the other hand, in the process of such a cultural translation, these values and principles cannot but be localized or metamorphosed, for cultural interpenetration always appears in international cultural communication, in the process of which translation plays a vital role. Homi Bhabha illustrates his new description of cultural translation in the context of global postcoloniality:

Translation is the performative nature of cultural communication. It is language *in actu* (enunciation, positionality) rather than language *in situ* (*enonce*, or propositionality). And the sign of translation continually tells, or "tolls" the different times and spaces between cultural authority and its performative practices. The "time" of translation consists of that *movement* of meaning, the principle and practice of a communication that, in the words of de Man "puts the original in motion to decanonize it, giving it the movement of fragmentation, a wandering of errance, a kind of permanent exile."[6]

Obviously, on the one hand, translation is still practised by means of language, but on the other hand, this means has enlarged its scope to that of culture or narration. That is to say, translation is usually done on the level of cross-cultural communication rather than mere language communication. That is why translation in our age is destined to play both the role of "colonizing" a national culture and the role of "decolonizing" it at the same time. Just as Edward Said has recently pointed out:

The gradual emergence in the humanities of confused and fragmented paradigms of research, such as those available through the new fields of postcolonial, ethnic, and other particularistic or identity-based study, reflects the eclipse of the old authoritative, Eurocentric models and the new ascendancy of a globalized, postmodern consciousness from which, as Benita Parry and others have argued, the gravity of history has been excised. Anticolonial liberation theory and the real history of empire, with its massacres and exploitation, have turned into a focus on the anxieties and ambivalences of the colonizer, the silent thereby colonized and displaced somehow.[7]

Apparently, the struggle between colonization and anti-colonization or decolonization has never ceased. That is why more and more translation scholars are interested in the topic of postcolonialism as it is relevant to translation practice; and from a postcolonial perspective, they can deal with some theoretical issues. In fact, confronted with the trend of cultural globalization, every culture has more or less been affected as, in influencing other cultures, it cannot avoid being influenced by other cultures; cultural interpenetration is thus inevitable. In the process of Chinese–Western cultural translation, Western cultural values and literary ideas, no matter how strong and influential they might be, cannot be understood well by Chinese readers unless they are expressed in idiomatic and understandable Chinese. In translating these cultural values and aesthetic ideas into idiomatic Chinese, a sort of localization or "decolonization" has largely been realized. For, according to Nida's concept of "dynamic equivalence", these ideas and values have already been shaped by Chinese linguistic and cultural conventions. And by and by, they will be "sinicized" and will finally become part of Chinese language and culture. For instance, the words of Western origin like "sofa", "coffee", "logic" and "taxi" (pronounced "*dishi*" in Cantonese but has now become widely used in all the cities of mainland China) have now been assimilated into the words frequently used by Chinese people or even included in Chinese dictionaries. Similarly, those English words of Chinese origin like "mahjong", "tofu" and "kung fu" have become widely used in the English-speaking world or even recognized by computer software.[8] Thus, we cannot jump to the conclusion that the translation of Western culture into Chinese is an act of "colonizing" Chinese language and culture, for something different appears at the same time.

I have pointed out elsewhere that from a cultural perspective, globalization will not necessarily homogenize all national cultures, for it has also brought about the diversity or plurality of culture. Thus, in the age of globalization, along with the migration of people from one place to another, national and cultural identity will also split into different identities. Speaking of her own "alien" Indian status in the United States and the Hindu heritage, the postcolonial critic Gayatri C. Spivak suggests in her recent book that "since the 'national origins' of the new immigrants, as fantasized by themselves, have not, so far, contributed to the unacknowledged and remoter historical culture of the United States, what we are demanding is that the United States recognize *our* rainbow as part of its history of the present".[9] So in the present era, cultural globalization is still opposed by the other stubborn and strong force— cultural localization—which finds particular embodiment in cultural translation. The fact is that both globalization and localization are equally dominant; the future orientation of world culture is one where the two trends are juxtaposed with one another. That is, we might "think globally", but "act locally". More specifically, a sort of cultural "glocalization" will appear in front of us. Since translation is done by human beings, it cannot avoid any type of "*alterity*", which sometimes may well produce some new significance in another cultural context: "In usual cultural explanations, classical and modern, the austere transcendentalization of alterity in Indic monism is made to coexist with these invaginated representations of the quick change into alterity by way of an argument from allegory."[10] But what factor will help us realize this goal? Obviously, it is translation, for translation, in its broadest sense, not only means "to change from one language into another", but also means "to change from one culture into another" by means of language. If it is true that, as Chinese intellectuals, we just place emphasis on the translation of Western languages into Chinese when we want to import anything advanced from the West, then when we have learned enough from the West to engage in equitable dialogue with our Western colleagues, we should have full reason to introduce our own culture to our Western colleagues through translation as most of our Western colleagues are not able to communicate with us in the Chinese language at the moment. If the former is still viewed by some people as a practice of cultural "colonization", then the latter should undoubtedly be regarded as a practice of cultural "decolonization". In this respect, we Chinese translators and translation scholars should undertake the task of "decolonizing" our culture and literature if they have really been "colonized" in the past.

9

Cultural Studies
in China

To discuss cultural studies in China, one should first of all make a clear distinction between what "culture" means in its traditional elite sense and in its contemporary form—the non-elite-oriented "cultural studies". For the former, I just use "culture studies" and for the latter, I follow the usage in current Western scholarship: "cultural studies". The present chapter will emphasize the latter although some space will be devoted to the former. In order for my Western colleagues to know more about how cultural studies is practised in the Chinese context—although in a different form—I will try to give a comprehensive picture of it as compared with its practice in the Western context.

REDEFINING CULTURAL STUDIES
IN THE CHINESE CONTEXT

Cultural studies, since its birth as a "sub-discipline" or an interdisciplinary academic discourse in the Western context, has been given different definitions by different scholars and numerous practitioners of this newly emergent discipline. Of all the definitions or descriptions, I would like to quote Simon During's early definition, for it is the most influential in the Chinese context and thus most relevant to what I am going to discuss in this chapter. To him, "cultural studies is not an academic discipline quite like others. It possesses neither a well-defined methodology nor clearly demarcated fields for investigation. Cultural studies is, of course, the study of culture, or, more particularly, the study of *contemporary* culture."[1] That is, "for cultural studies, 'culture' was not an abbreviation of a 'high culture' assumed to have constant value across time and space".[2] Judging by this, we can sum it up as follows: Cultural studies as will be discussed here is chiefly a study of the different "cultural phenomena" occurring around us which are both dynamic and energetic rather than a study of those elite "cultural products" described in books. From this, we can easily see its anti-aesthetic, anti-disciplinary, anti-institutional and popular culture-oriented features.

Obviously, in talking about cultural studies in the present era, we cannot but think of the strong impact of globalization on contemporary Chinese literary and cultural production and representation, for this impact is so strong that it is beyond anyone's expectation and resistance. Since I am a Chinese scholar doing both literary and culture studies in general, I will focus here on the current Chinese literary and cultural situation as I think it might prove the internal and external connections between globalization and literature and culture in the present time. In this way, it is necessary to first of all observe the case of contemporary Chinese society.

Cultural studies in China is by no means a contingent event, for it is based on the theoretical debate on postmodernism and the birth of various postmodern theories in the Chinese context in the latter part of the 1980s. Since the beginning of the 1990s, China has been in the process of building a market economy in a broader context of global and transnational capitalization, which cannot but have affected the studies of culture and literature. The Chinese government has always maintained the strategy that, politically, it should continue to take the road of socialism, or a sort of socialism of "Chinese characteristics", but on the other hand, it does welcome foreign investment if it is limited to the domain of the economy and finances without influencing Chinese culture. Actually, we cannot avoid the fact that the investment of foreign capital cannot but influence the production of literature and culture, with the effects most conspicuous in China's film production and film studies. As compared to literary creation, Chinese film, due to the intervention of transnational investment and the advent of postmodern consumerism, has taken the first step toward the world stage with Zhang Yimou and Chen Kaige being awarded various international film prizes. But in the field of literary production, no domestic Chinese writer—if Gao Xingjian is regarded as a French-Chinese writer—has received the elusive Nobel Prize for literature since literary production, especially in the age of globalization and under the impact of cultural studies, is distancing itself farther and farther away from consumer culture as well as the study of it, or cultural studies.

In the face of the strong impact of the market economy as a direct consequence of economic globalization, consumer culture has become one of the hot topics confronting Chinese scholars of both literary and cultural studies. The introduction of cultural studies is more or less connected with the rise of popular culture and studies on contemporary consumer culture. Apparently, the culture characterized as being manufactured, commercial and consumptive undoubtedly destroys the elegance and sublimity of elite culture and its products, literature and art. The attempt to redefine culture appears now and then in some scholarly books of humanistic spirit, but the attention given to consumer culture in China is strikingly different from the great importance attached to it in Western academic circles. Popular culture or consumer culture has always been severely criticized as something unhealthy and something that rebels against the traditional humanistic spirit in current Chinese critical circles. But ironically speaking, popular culture or consumer culture has indeed permeated our daily cultural and intellectual life and even academic research and cultural production, challenging our elite and canonical sense of literature and art. Scholars of literature and art cannot but be confronted with such questions: How should we face the severe challenge raised by the rise of popular culture? What will be the future of canonical literature and art since we are now in the age of globalization when information is spreading very swiftly and across boundaries? Should we still maintain the binary opposition between elite culture and popular culture in such an age of globalization when the situation is more favourable for the production of popular culture and literature, as these are more welcomed by the broad masses of people? This is what China's cultural studies scholars have been confronted with at first. That is, cultural studies has started to undergo a sort of "redefinition" or "relocation" in the Chinese context like its precursors, postmodernism and postcolonialism.[3]

As we all know, exploring consumer culture in the West was not merely an event in the 1990s. Early in the discussion on the issue of postmodernism launched in the circles of American culture and literary theory, quite a few critics had already touched upon consumer culture in the post-industrial society in an attempt to "cross the border" between high culture and low culture and "close the gap" between canonical literature and popular literature. Leslie Fiedler and many others, standing at the forefront of defending the legitimacy of popular culture, once tried to narrow the artificial gap between elite culture and popular culture. His insightful observation actually anticipated the later study and critique of postmodernism made by Fredric Jameson and other Western Marxist critics.[4] It also paved the way more or less for the later rise of cultural criticism and cultural studies in North American academic circles, which deal in a theoretical way with popular culture and consumer culture. The reason why the modernist elite culture is severely challenged in the contemporary era is simply because it confines itself to the isolated ivory tower; it is incompatible with the broad masses of audience (consumers of culture and art), and is hardly able to escape the unfavourable situation. Postmodernism, however, tries in a flexible way to bridge the gap between high culture and popular culture tactfully. But because it is decentralization- and plurality-oriented, postmodernism would bring about an obscure and relative standard with which to judge the value of art. As a result, duplicated art and pastiched art appear, made with high technology and characterized by depthlessness, plainness, multiplicity, collage and fragmentariness. The appearance of all the above has certainly attracted the attention of scholars and theorists who have a strong social responsibility, but their concern does not merely lie in their opposition to these phenomena, but rather in their effort to confront these complicated phenomena so as to anatomize them from the perspective of cultural studies. Through these analyses and interpretations, they could probably offer some practical strategies. I think of it as a positive attitude, the result of which will not intensify the established opposition between the two types of culture but will help them to co-exist and complement each other.

In the current Chinese cultural and intellectual context, some humanities scholars and cultural and literary critics are very much worried about the prevalence of consumer culture and art in recent years, trying to oppose its challenge by "saving the crisis of the humanistic spirit". This is not hard to imagine. But consequently, it might well intensify the existing opposition between high culture and popular culture. In a society where the market economy is gradually becoming dominant according to the laws and regulations of the WTO, such opposition will undoubtedly lead to the death of elite culture and art if it is distanced from the broad masses of people. The fact is that consumer culture does occupy an important place in contemporary China, dominating cultural production and communication like a hidden God. So if we realize the legitimacy of its existence and make proper use of it, it would probably help produce high cultural products; otherwise, it would gradually swallow the already shrinking cultural market. Along with China's recent entry into the WTO, this consequence will become clearer to us scholars of literary and cultural studies. Since China's contemporary cultural production is closely related to economic development, it is also necessary for us to be aware of what cultural studies are going on in the West or elsewhere. I think the above description may well help our Western colleagues to have a better understanding of how and in what atmosphere cultural studies was introduced into China and how it has flourished in recent years.

Since the beginning of the 1990s, China's socialist-plan economy has been shifting toward a market economy, and the country has been in transition with respect to politics, economics and culture, with different forces and discourses co-existing and complementing each other; some scholars are still exploring cultural theory proper and its value in the academic circles, with the objective of a conscious construction of Chinese cultural theory; international cultural exchanges have made it possible for Chinese–Western academic communication and theoretical dialogue to take place; the production of high cultural products in the form of literature and art occurs under the conditions of a market economy, with the *avant-garde* productions fading away; and the rise of consumer culture, which is developing in a pluralistically oriented direction, challenges traditional elite culture and the humanities. But on the other hand, some publishing houses still try to publish excellent canonical literary works in perfectly designed form; that is, serious literature and art can still be produced in a popular way, but the effect is not always conspicuous. In light of all this, what strategy should we adopt? I think that the cultural studies scholars in contemporary China have really done something practical and effective. So it is necessary here to summarize briefly the positive impacts of the introduction of cultural studies since the beginning of the 1990s.

THE RISE OF CULTURAL STUDIES IN CHINA AS A NEW CRITICAL AND THEORETICAL DISCOURSE

Among today's Chinese scholars, there is still some confusion between cultural studies in its contemporary sense and cultural studies in its traditional sense. Actually, cultural studies, as a newly rising branch of learning and a prevailing interdisciplinary discourse, was first introduced in China at the beginning of the 1990s, immediately after the introduction and translation of various Western postmodern theories and postcolonial cultural trends, with such journals as *Dushu* (Reading), *Wenyi bao* (Literature and Art Gazette), *Guowai wenxue* (Foreign Literatures), *Wenyi yanjiu* (Literature and Art Studies), *Wenxue pinglun* (Literary

Review) and *Tongsu wenxue pinglun* (Review of Popular Literature) enthusiastically pushing forward its development in the Chinese context. I should say that cultural studies in China has now undergone three major stages: (1) origination and introduction through translation; (2) establishment of an international dialogue and intercultural exchange; and (3) institutionalization and "glocalization". Since the development of cultural studies is still in full swing in the Chinese context at the moment, my account will stop at the year 2002.

Like the origin and development of postmodernism and postcolonialism as cultural trends and critical theories in China, the rise of cultural studies in the Chinese context chiefly resulted from the critical introduction and creative reception by some *avant-garde* Chinese scholars who mainly based their activities in Beijing and Shanghai. In a broader Chinese context, cultural studies rose almost simultaneously in the three regions of China: in Taiwan, with the National Tsing Hua University as the very centre; in Hong Kong, with the enthusiastic advocation by scholars at the University of Hong Kong and Lingnan University; and in the mainland, first centred at Peking University and now centred at Tsinghua University. I will focus on the practice of cultural studies in mainland China.

The first essay introducing cultural studies in a Chinese journal was entitled "Dazhong wenhua he wenhua yanjiu" ("Popular Culture and Cultural Studies") and was published in the influential *Wenyi bao* (Literature and Art Gazette) on 19 February 1994.[5] For the first time, it connects the study of contemporary popular culture and consumer culture with the new approach of cultural studies, thus informing Chinese scholars of the difference compared to traditional cultural studies of elite cultural phenomena. Immediately after the publication of this first short essay, a longer introductory essay written by the American sinologist of Chinese origin, Leo Lee, entitled "Shenme shi 'wenhua yanjiu'" ("What is 'Cultural Studies'?") was published successively in the seventh and eighth issues of the widely read intellectual journal *Dushu* (Reading) in 1994. The enthusiastic introduction and comments on this newly rising interdisciplinary research method and critical discourse in the West marked the origin and then the steady development of cultural studies in mainland China. But its initial introduction was overshadowed by two other more heatedly discussed topics borrowed from Western academic circles: postmodernism, which was already showing its decline, and postcolonialism, which attracted more attention from Chinese critical circles then as an emergent force after the decline of postmodernism. So in the first stage, cultural studies was discussed and practised in a comparatively narrow academic and critical domain with the involvement of few scholars.

However, it immediately aroused the interest of some scholars who were teaching or doing research in Beijing and Shanghai. Wang Hui, who was then a research fellow in the Institute of Literature at the Chinese Academy of Social Sciences and now a professor at Tsinghua University, played an active part in the introduction and practice of cultural studies in China. Since his editorship in the late 1990s, he, together with his co-editor, Huang Ping, has gradually made the journal *Dushu* a prestigious journal of cultural criticism and studies in general. The years 1995 to 1999 saw the rapid development and flourishing of cultural studies in China, with almost all the major young literary scholars and cultural critics enthusiastically involved in it. One of the culminating achievements made in China's cultural studies at this stage, from an international point of view, was the International Conference on Cultural Studies: China and the West, held in Dalian in August 1995. Such internationally renowned scholars in the field of literary and cultural studies as Ralph Cohen, Terry Eagleton and Jonathan Arac attended the conference and gave plenary speeches. Quite a few overseas Chinese scholars, such as Henry Y. H. Zhao, Liu Kang, Sheldon Lu and Shaobo Xie, intervened in the Chinese critical circles, which immediately bridged the gap between the domestic and overseas Chinese scholarship, especially in the areas of postmodern, postcolonial and cultural studies. A correspondent from the influential BBC was also present at the conference and interviewed the conference organizers, Wang Ning and Ralph Cohen. As a result of the conference, a special issue of the internationally prestigious journal, *New Literary History*, was published which presented before the international scholarship the state of the art of cultural studies in the broad Chinese context, although at the time, few Chinese scholars had a clear idea of cultural studies in its contemporary sense. Some eight articles delivered at the Dalian conference were also published in Chinese in the journal, *Guowai wenxue*, in early 1996. After the Dalian conference, cultural studies immediately became a very energetic new branch of learning in China, attracting more and more eminent scholars and critics, and engaging them in this stimulating and interesting field. Those publishing extensively in this field include myself, Wang Hui, Dai Jinhua, Chen Xiaoming, Zhang Yiwu, Wang Yichuan, Wang Yuechuan, Huang Ping, Ye Shuxian, Tao Dongfeng, Jin Yuanpu, Zhou Xian, Yang Naiqiao,

Wang Min'an, Luo Gang, Wang Fengzhen, Gao Bingzhong, Zhao Bin, Yin Hong, Mao Sihui and Chen Yongguo. Although most of these scholars used to be engaged in the study of literary theory, comparative literature or contemporary Chinese literature, their recent publications indeed cover a wide range of disciplines including anthropology, sociology, communication, gender studies and postcolonial studies. I should say that this stage marked the prime of cultural studies in China, during which Chinese scholars of cultural studies engaged in equitable dialogue with the international scholarship. And quite a few eminent Western scholars in the relevant fields were invited to visit China either for conferences or for lectures, including Homi Bhabha, Arif Dirlik, Perry Anderson, Simon During, Ien Ang, Michael Taussig, David Birch, Dudley Andrew and Roland Robertson. Other scholars, whose major areas of study include literary theory or comparative literature, were also invited to exchange views with their Chinese counterparts, including Fredric Jameson, J. Hillis Miller, Terry Eagleton, Douwe Fokkema, Lawrence Buell, Emory Elliott, Tom Mitchell, Theo D'haen, Michael Holquist, Paul Bové, John Frow, Gabriel Schwab, Iain Chambers, Rien Segers and Lindsay Waters. All the above-mentioned scholars, in their lectures or conference speeches, more or less touch upon areas such as cultural identity studies, gender studies, posthuman studies, ecocriticism, aesthetic ideology, media studies, diasporic studies and lesbian studies, which actually cover a wide range of issues discussed in current international cultural studies circles.

If we say that the second stage marked the increasing maturity of cultural studies in China, then the third stage saw its institutionalization and curriculum planning in Chinese academia and universities, although in the West, cultural studies is still characterized by being anti-theory and anti-institutionalization. In this respect, I should say that the development of cultural studies in China is almost on the same level as that in the Western context, and sometimes even more advanced than that in the West. For in Western academic circles, there are still quite a number of literary scholars who are strongly opposed to the prevalence of cultural studies. But in China, such senior literary scholars as Yue Daiyun and Qian Zhongwen are still interested in the recent development of cultural studies at home and abroad and they try to publish some excellent essays in their edited journals or book series.[6] A new milestone in China's cultural studies was the founding and publication of the journal, *Wenhua yanjiu* (Cultural Studies), as a book series in Tianjin at the beginning of the twenty-first century.[7] Like the rise of cultural studies in the English-speaking world, the editorial department of the journal in China is also located at the "periphery"—the Capital Normal University in Beijing—rather than the international prestigious academic "centre"— Peking University or Tsinghua University, or the Chinese Academy of Social Sciences. With the joint efforts made by literary scholars, sociologists, anthropologists and communication scholars, cultural studies in China has developed into a very promising new discipline and a dynamic critical discourse which will help restructure the established university curriculum and division of traditional disciplines and branches of learning in the humanities and social sciences. Unlike its opposition to comparative literature in Western academic circles, its practice has proved that it can at least co-exist with literary studies, especially with a cross-cultural study of Chinese–Western comparative literature. The current practice is actually developing in this direction although it is sometimes criticized by some literary scholars subscribing to traditional elite literary doctrines.

At present, we can easily show that the range and content of cultural studies in China are similar to those in Western academic circles. It covers at least four areas: ethnic studies, including studies of postcolonial, minority and diasporic writing; area studies, including Asian studies and Pacific studies; gender studies, including studies of female and gay and lesbian writings; and media studies, including film, TV and even Internet studies. And the mapping of cultural studies in China's capital, Beijing, is jointly made by different groups of scholars: At Peking University, Dai Jinhua's film studies from the cultural perspective co-exist with Zhang Yiwu's dynamic cultural interpretation and analysis of contemporary Chinese literary culture and consumer cultural phenomena; and Gao Bingzhong is still doing field research in some remote or even minority regions rather than merely staying in the academic centre, Beijing. At Tsinghua University, Wang Ning and the Centre for Comparative Literature and Cultural Studies try to combine the two academic branches of comparative literature and cultural studies—with both "culture" in its elite sense and "cultures" in their contemporary sense—in an attempt to make it possible for cultural studies to communicate with comparative literature studies and even translation studies. At the recent International Conference on Translation and Interdisciplinary Studies (2002), co-sponsored by Tsinghua University and Lingnan University of Hong Kong, participants from Asia, Europe and North America discussed such issues of interdisciplinary fields as translation and anthropology, translation in the context of cultural studies, the function of translation in the age of globalization, translation and postcoloniality, translation and cultural construction, and even translation of the body. Thus, translation studies has actually been placed in the broad context of cultural studies. At the Tsinghua–Harvard Symposium on Postcolonialism held on 25 June 2002, Homi Bhabha was invited to give a keynote speech in which he not only addressed issues of identity studies in the global postcolonial context, but also put forward his more ambitious project of "minoritization", which to him will be another type of globalization. At Renmin University of China, Jin Yuanpu attaches more importance to the increasing urbanization of Beijing and its cultural production associated with the humanization of the 2008 Olympic Games to be held in Beijing. At the Capital Normal University, Tao Dongfeng and Yang Naiqiao conduct their research on culture from the postcolonial perspective and that of cultural identity studies, although Yang seems to be more concerned about the reconstruction of comparative literature in a broad cross-cultural context. In the Chinese Academy of Social Sciences, Ye Shuxian still maintains his position of cultural anthropology in an attempt to "emancipate" the "repressed" and "marginal" cultural phenomena in China's broad rural and minority areas. In Shanghai, Nanjing and Guangzhou, quite a few literary scholars and cultural critics have become interested in this newly rising academic approach and try to practise it in order to broaden the scope of their literary studies and criticism. In this respect, Zhou Xian's recent editorial and writing practice indicates that cultural studies has also permeated Chinese scholars' academic consciousness and anticipates the establishment of yet another centre in Nanjing. In Shanghai, Chen Sihe, who used to be engaged in the rewriting of modern Chinese literary history, now focuses on the issue of civic society and popular writing in Shanghai in the 1930s. In Guangzhou, Mao Sihui, who is now teaching in Macau, organized two international conferences in 2001 and 2002 on British and American literary and cultural studies while he was teaching in Guangzhou, at which direct academic dialogue was carried out in English between Chinese and Western scholarship. Along with the increasing interest in globalization and its relationship with culture, these scholars have involved themselves increasingly in the study of globalization and its positive and negative effects on the construction of Chinese culture and literary studies. They are undoubtedly the leaders in the current trends of Chinese cultural and literary studies in general and shoulder the task of continuing dialogues with their Western and international counterparts.

TOWARD A SORT OF CULTURAL STUDIES OF CHINESE CHARACTERISTICS

In illustrating the characteristics of China's Marxism and socialism, both Mao Zedong and Deng Xiaoping have made great contributions, the central part of which is characterized by pragmatism and practicality. That is, putting the Marxist doctrine (brought in from the West) in the local context of the Chinese revolution led to the successful founding of the People's Republic of China in 1949. Similarly, the drastic change in the past 20 years in China has also proved that without localizing Western (socialist) theory in the Chinese context, there would be no achievements made in China's socialist construction, which has already incorporated many elements of Western capitalism since we are now in an age of global capitalization. In discussing cultural studies and its practice in the Chinese context, I have, in the previous sections, chiefly discussed cultural studies in its contemporary sense in an attempt to place it in a broad cross-cultural and global context. But actually, in the Chinese context, cultural studies in its traditional sense is more widely practised by scholars other than those in literary studies. I highlight some aspects here: Quite a few Chinese films directed by Zhang Yimou, Chen Kaige and others have won awards in international film festivals, thus advancing China's film production and film studies in a global context; the central and local governments have attached great importance to traditional Chinese theatre, such as the Peking Opera and many other local operas, in an attempt to resist the penetration of foreign, especially Western, culture; and quite a few classical Chinese and foreign literary works have been issued with new versions or editions so that they can satisfy the needs of the broad masses of reading public.

Due to the joint efforts made by these two groups of scholars, current Chinese cultural studies has taken on a new look which is different from its counterpart in the West. We could also say that we are now moving toward the construction of a sort of culture studies of Chinese characteristics. This sort of cultural studies will not only incorporate many of the issues discussed and being discussed in current cultural studies in the West but also combine studies of cultural issues and phenomena in the Chinese context, such as traditional Chinese culture and its products

(Peking Opera) and contemporary Chinese culture and its products (performing arts, film and TV) since culture, in general, is wide in scope and inclusive in connotation. Only by maintaining such an open and pluralistic attitude can we push China's cultural studies forward and enable it to engage in exchanges and equitable dialogue with the international cultural studies scholarship.

Whitman and Modernity: Translation and Reception of Whitman in Modern Chinese Literature

In the current era, confronted by economic globalization, cultural globalization and mass media globalization, literature and other forms of elite culture are becoming more and more marginalized along with the depression of the cultural and literary market. But why are we still discussing Walt Whitman, an American romantic poet in the late nineteenth century, who should certainly be regarded as being representative of elite culture and literature with a strong *avant-garde* flavour? This is perhaps what I want to address on this occasion. To my understanding, the very significance of Whitman today does not only lie in the influential role he played in the era of globalization, but also in his aesthetic spirit that is relevant to this era in which works of art are manufactured without careful elaboration and artistic imagination. Upon thinking of Whitman, we cannot but recollect his adventures in literary exploration and powerful imagination in the latter part of the nineteenth century, and the unique role he and his poetry played in the development of Western and Chinese modernity with regard to postmodernity and the historic *avant-garde*. It is true that Walt Whitman as well as his poetry has undoubtedly heralded the advent of experimental poetry during the peak of Western modernist literature and the May 4th period in China, with the latter being strongly influenced by the former. Actually, as a great gifted experimentalist and poetic innovator himself, Whitman, with his remarkable poetry and powerful poetic discourse, has indeed influenced the development of political and cultural modernity both in the West and in China. Since modernity is still a heatedly discussed and

117

debated topic in the era of globalization, in order to discuss Whitman in a comparative context of both Western and Chinese literature, he and his poetry should first of all be placed in the framework of modernity.

MODERNIZING WHITMAN: THE WEST AND CHINA

Whitman has long been regarded as a romantic poet, or a democratic fighter in American history. But in this chapter, I will only reflect on him and his poetry by putting him in the framework of modernity, or modernizing him and his poetry from today's point of view. It is true that literary modernism is a sort of transcendence over romanticism, to which various kinds of writers in the nineteenth century contributed a great deal. In speaking of the pioneers of modernism, we usually mention Edgar Allan Poe (poetry), Henrik Ibsen (drama) and Gustave Flaubert (novels). It is sad that most of the twentieth-century literary scholars, partly due to their overlook of the rise of American literature in the latter part of the nineteenth century, and partly due to their stubborn sense of Eurocentrism, seem to have forgotten another important figure from the United States whose literary works were still overshadowed by English literature then—Walt Whitman. It was this great figure who, with poetry as his trumpet, uttered a strong voice of democracy both in politics as well as in aesthetics in the latter part of the nineteenth century. So we often say that the basic tone of Whitman's poetry is that of romanticism, but a later romanticism with a sort of premodern code in aesthetic exploration. Among all the scholars of literary modernism, Malcolm Bradbury and James McFarlane are probably two of the very few insightful scholars who have observed the pioneering role played by Whitman in the process of European modernism: "When the German writers of the late 1880s thought of 'modern' literature, of whom did *they* think? Of Ibsen, of Zola and Tolstoy, Daudt, Bret Harte, and Whitman."[1] All these writers either provided inspiration to the modernists or were themselves pioneers of modernist literature. In Western academic circles, scholars of different critical orientations have highly appreciated Whitman's artistic achievements or worldwide impact. Some scholars regard him as "one of the pioneering figures in modern poetry" or the "innovator of modern free verse", simply because his works helped to forge a sort of American national and cultural identity and form a strong American voice in world literary circles. They have also found his democratic spirit and endless search for the true identity of the American nation relevant to the historic *avant-garde* of twentieth-century literature.[2] If we read his poetry carefully in regard to some of the contemporary American experimentalist poets, we can undoubtedly find the inherent connections between him and those postmodern poets.[3] That is perhaps one of the reasons why he is still read and discussed in today's postmodern context.

Obviously, the reason why we Chinese scholars still discuss Whitman in regard to modern Chinese literature is also due to the unique role that he played in the development of China's political and cultural modernity as well as in the literary modernist movement. As is well-known, during the May 4th period, Whitman was one of the very few American poets who had a strong impact on such revolutionary Chinese poets as Guo Moruo, Hu Shi, Tian Han, Xu Zhimo, Wen Yiduo, Liu Bannong, Ai Qing and others, who either translated his poems into Chinese or conscientiously drew upon his writings in their works.[4] His democratic spirit and pioneering sense of aesthetic adventure inherent in his poetry were translated into a forceful stimulus for the nascent Chinese literature. As the critical and creative reception of Whitman's poetry was absolutely relevant to the then Chinese social revolution and literary innovation as well as the cultural and receptive circumstances, his work was translated and classified in the tradition of nineteenth-century romanticism for a long time. But according to the recent advances made in Western academic circles, Whitman is discussed more as a pioneering figure of literary modernism than merely as a romantic poet, for his appearance in the nineteenth century actually heralded the later rise of modernist poetry in the twentieth century, and many of his prophetic and insightful ideas actually paved the way for the development of modernity in both Western culture and thinking. Inspired by this, I would like to re-explore Whitman and his poetic writing in regard to his translation and critical and creative reception in China from the perspective of modernity.

As is well-known, analyzing Whitman and his poetry from the perspective of modernist theory is by no means a recent undertaking in Western academic circles. To my mind, however, the reason why Whitman and his works are still favourably appreciated and studied by scholars is largely due to the fact that his poems are of more than one code. They obviously have different cultural and aesthetic codes. That is, apart from the romantic and realistic codes, there are several other codes which are, of course, of certain critical value. Through my careful observations, I can affirm that among other possible literary and cultural

119

codes, modernism or modernity might well be one of the most important codes which make his writings still relevant to the current theoretical debate about modernity and postmodernity. In speaking of the characteristics of contemporary postmodernist literature, Douwe Fokkema sums it up as follows: "...In Postmodernism, the most 'democratic' of all literary codes, the role of the reader is emphasized even more than in Modernism."[5] Since Whitman's poetry has more than one code, the reader could find some new significance far beyond romanticism. His poetic writing not only inspired modernist writers, but also postmodernist writers. We can easily find his symbolic description of sex in his *Leaves of Grass* which certainly inspired T. S. Eliot, who developed and parodied this theme in his *The Waste Land* in the twentieth century, representing a different spirit of time from what Whitman eulogizes in his poetry. If the tone in Whitman's work is highly enthusiastic and sublime, then in Eliot's work, the major tone is much more profound and sad which brings the reader deep into meditation. We can also find his influence and echo in Allen Ginsberg's beat poems in the post-war years, with the elements of destruction of all the old things highlighted. Whether they admit or not, these writers of the later generations cannot but regard Whitman as one of the possible sources of their creative inspiration. With the passing of time, we have no difficulty in finding that many of the issues Whitman touched upon over a century ago are still being discussed in the present age in which modernity, to many people, has not yet ended although it is severely challenged by those who advocate postmodernity.[6] We should say that, like Ibsen, Whitman wrote for a rising people and society, eulogizing an aggressive and ambitious nation whose identity is very conspicuous. That is, he wrote not only for his own age, but also for the future. So it is not surprising that in his lifetime, his views were incompatible with those of the critical circles and were even severely attacked by those short-sighted critics. Now all those who attacked Whitman are completely forgotten by contemporary people, but he himself and his poems are still discussed by present-day scholars and literary critics both in the West and in China.

When we discuss Whitman in terms of modernity, we should first of all confront the very problem that different scholars have different definitions about the concept of modernity. It is both viewed as a literary and art spirit in its broadest aesthetic sense as well as a cultural project of enlightenment in its broadest political, cultural and intellectual sense. But I should distinguish between modernity and modernism, with the former referring to a cultural and intellectual state or a project and the latter referring to a literary and art movement or an aesthetic spirit and principle representing a dominant cultural and aesthetic trend in a given time. It is also true that different scholars may define modernism differently, but many of them view it chiefly as a European cultural and literary movement.[7] Thus, it is not strange that Whitman is regarded as one of the pioneering figures of modernist literature, both in thinking and in artistic innovation. In my view, the role played by Whitman in the development of Western modernity manifests itself both in the field of cultural and intellectual enlightenment as well as that of literary innovation; his symbolic descriptions of erotic love certainly offer the Freudian psychoanalytic critics precious material for analysis, and his breakthrough with conventional poetic diction opens broad possibilities of writing modern poetry, and great importance is attached to his eulogy of nature by contemporary ecocritics. That is perhaps the very reason why many of the writers who were once as well-known as Whitman are not remembered by contemporary people while Whitman still stands out from his era. I should say that as long as modernity is still a stimulating and fascinating theoretical topic attracting contemporary scholars, Whitman and his poetry will not be out of fashion, for it is Whitman who has played an important role in shaping European, American and Chinese modernity.

Like other great writers, Whitman is undoubtedly unique, both in literary ideals and artistic devices. His purpose, in his own well-known words, is "mainly...to put a *Person*, a human being (myself, in the latter half of the Nineteenth Century, in America,) freely, fully and truly on record". He was therefore "the bard of personality", speaking for all Americans (and for all mankind), since he knew that all other human beings were essentially the same as himself. That is also one of the main reasons why his poetry not only helped to form a sort of American national spirit and identity but is itself filled with humanistic sense in general. So his legacy does not just belong to America, but rather to the whole world. All the sympathetic feelings for human beings and many other ingredients went into the first edition of *Leaves of Grass*. In his 1855 preface to *Leaves of Grass*, Whitman declares that "of all mankind the great poet is the equable man". The same phrase recurs in "By Blue Ontario's Shore", and it is the word "equable" that best sums up the peculiar temper of

Whitman. Democracy and freedom are translated and symbolized by the humblest of natural growths—the grass which grows freely. To him, the idea that life is the precise structure of classical architecture is a fiction. Rather, it is like an object in nature, with an organic form that is nevertheless unexpected, asymmetrical, and even wilful. To him, speaking of himself conceals "his rhythm and uniformity...in the roots of his verse, not to be seen of themselves, but to break forth loosely as lilacs on a bush, and take shapes compact, as the shapes of melons, or chestnuts, or pears". Thus, Whitman's view of the poet, which was different from many of his contemporaries, is of one who "judges not as the judge, judges but as the sun falling around a helpless thing". Obviously, like any other poet's theory of the function of a poet, this is a personal testament. Whitman himself is close not only to human beings but also to nature itself as is indicated both in the manifest meaning of grass itself and its latent significance. He tries in his poetry to bridge the gap between nature and the human world by "beautifying" or "symbolizing" nature. He wrote about mankind and sang of nature as he loved them both. For him, if the poet cannot speak *to* mankind, he can at least speak *for* mankind. This is how Whitman's poetry represents the very spirit of time when the American nation was newly born and developing energetically like the wildly growing grass. Even in the early twentieth century, when romanticism had already been replaced by modernism in literature, the American nation was still in a state of growth, and American literature was seldom filled with the sense of *fin de siècle*. Whitman felt the pulse of the nation and precisely grasped the right spirit of the time and thus predicted the future.

WHITMAN AND MODERN CHINESE LITERATURE REVISITED

In dealing with Whitman's significance in American literature, James Miller correctly regards him as an Adamic singer, and his *Leaves of Grass* an Adamic song,[8] for his poetry feels the very pulse of the spirit of the time, both culturally and aesthetically. It should also be pointed out that Whitman, along with many other Western writers, has indeed exerted a considerable influence on quite a few modern Chinese writers and intellectuals, especially with his experimentation with free verse, which even helped to popularize China's New Poetry movement at the time. Since these writers, such as Guo Moruo and Hu Shi, are major figures of

122

modern Chinese literature, this influence has actually helped in the rewriting of modern Chinese literary history, especially poetry.

Compared to what has been achieved in Western academic circles, I should say rather frankly that Whitman studies in China has been conducted in a very different orientation: He has been introduced and studied in China as merely a romanticist, or more exactly, a revolutionary romanticist, with his poems of social change inadequately highlighted and those of symbolism more or less neglected. This is largely due to the "dynamic" translation and "creative" reception by Chinese translators and writers. Although the mysterious and symbolic elements in his poems are sometimes mentioned, they are just dealt with in a brief way without being profoundly analyzed. This must be quite relevant to the cultural and intellectual atmosphere at the time when Whitman was first translated and introduced in China, as his works were very instrumental to China's modernity and new literary movement. That was in the time of the significant May 4th Movement which marked not only the beginning of new Chinese literature but also the very beginning of Chinese modernity. During that time, China needed something or someone from outside of the country to help promote its cultural and literary revolution. Since some of the major revolutionary writers or intellectuals, such as Guo Moruo and Hu Shi, loved Whitman's poetry and writing style, and appreciated his democratic spirit and enthusiastic attitude toward new things, Whitman became one of the very few Western writers who were regarded as cultural and intellectual idols by the Chinese.

As far as Chinese modernity is concerned, I will spend some time in describing the characteristics that are different from what appeared in the Western cultural context. Since Chinese intellectuals are famous for "grabbism", they grab everything from abroad for their own use, which finds particular embodiment in the significant May 4th period when almost all the Western trends of culture and literary thought were introduced and metamorphosed, through translation, in the Chinese context. So dealing with modern Chinese literature from the comparative perspective of influence–reception studies is an important strategy in rewriting modern Chinese literary history.[9] First of all, we should admit that even if Chinese modernity exists, it is still something translated and introduced from the West although it does represent, to a large extent, the internal logic of the development of modern Chinese culture and thinking. Thus, like the modernity in other regions, Chinese modernity, as part of the global trend of modernity, is characterized by its totality and enlightenment function. Since Chinese intellectuals in the May 4th period attached great importance to science and democracy, with which they could enlighten ordinary people, they enthusiastically welcomed Whitman's powerful and democratic poetics as well as his poetry. Although Poe and Whitman were two of the most frequently translated and mentioned American poets at the time, according to readily available research data, Whitman is only ranked seventh as a poet, after Shakespeare, Dryden, Goethe, Milton, Hugo and James the First.[10]

Although I will not trace the origin of the translation and introduction of Whitman in modern China in detail as this has already been done by many others, I should mention some important facts before exploring Whitman's inherent connection with, and significance for, Chinese modernity and China's literary modernism. During the May 4th period, along with the enthusiastic translation and introduction of Western literary thought and creative writing, Whitman was one of the very few American authors who attracted attention from China's translation circles, literary world and critical circles. In July 1919, three months after the significant May 4th Movement, the *avant-garde* journal, *Shaonian Zhongguo* (Young China), was launched, which certainly marked the beginning of the extensive translation of Western poetry in modern China. In the first issue of the journal, Tian Han, author of China's *National Anthem*, published a long article entitled "Pingmin shiren huiteman de bainian ji" ("Centennial Commemoration of People's Poet Whitman"). In this article, he not only introduces Whitman's life and work but lays particular emphasis on his democratic thoughts and aesthetic ideas.[11] Obviously, to Tian and other Chinese intellectuals and writers at the time, the greatest significance of Whitman for modern China—or "young" China to Tian—as well as its literature does not merely lie in his innovation in literary form which is undoubtedly necessary but more importantly in his democratic thought inherent in his poetry, which is one of the two most stimulating factors—Mr. De (democracy) and Mr. Sai (science)—speeding up the development of China's cultural and intellectual modernity. In another literary journal, *Shi* (Poetry), which was published in seven issues, Whitman, together with the Imagist poets, was among the most important Western poets who deserved to be translated and introduced to the Chinese audience. In order to save space, I will just mention a few of the names in this chapter.

According to the readily available research results and my further investigation, Guo Moruo was the very Chinese writer who was most profoundly influenced by Whitman or who derived the most inspiration from his master. Like Whitman, Guo hated all those who might bind his imagination in literary creation, in an attempt to freely express his individuality. Thus, "he received influences from Tagore, Shelley, Heine, Goethe and Whitman, especially Whitman's 'wild and violent' poetry. Through drawing upon foreign poetry and his own creative transmutation, he formed a new poetic form characterized by both originality and traditional Chinese style."[12] Due to Guo's dominant position and wide influence in China's literary circles during the May 4th period and later, Whitman's reputation and influence in China was far greater than many of his contemporaries. What should be particularly mentioned here is that Guo himself was even regarded as "China's Whitman", which he himself never denied, but expressed his indebtedness to the latter frankly: "When I approached Whitman's *Leaves of Grass*, that was the year of the May 4th Movement. The repression of my feeling and that of the whole nation now found the outlet and the way of release. At the time I was almost paranoiac."[13] Guo's indebtedness to Whitman and admiration for him find particular embodiment in his great work *Nüshen* (Goddesses) which is usually recognized as one of the modern classics in Chinese literature and which highlights a sort of Whitmanian freedom and democracy by eulogizing his self and nature. He says rather frankly:

> Whitman's poetic style characterized by getting rid of all the conventions coincides with the spirit of *Sturm und Drang* of the May 4th period. I was totally shocked by his grand and eloquent tone. Influenced by him...I wrote all these poems full of masculine violence: "*Lizai diqiu bianshang de fanghao*" ("Trumpet Standing on the Edge of the Earth"), "*Diqiu, wode muqin*" ("Earth, My Mother"), "*Feitu song*" ("Song of the Bandits"), "*Chen an*" ("Good Morning"), "*Fenghuang niepan*" ("Nirvana of Phoenix"), "*Tian gou*" ("Heavenly Dog"), "*Xin deng*" ("Heart-lamp"), "*Lu zhong mei*" ("Coal in the Stove") and "*Ju pao zhi jiaoxun*" ("Lesson of the Huge Gun").[14]

It is true that Guo Moruo is one of the very few modern Chinese poets who have contributed to both China's cultural and intellectual modernity as well as its modernist literature. Since he derived the most inspiration from Whitman, the latter's contributions to China's modernity are therefore more conspicuous than those of most of the other Western writers.

If we regard Guo Moruo as a poet and that his contribution lies chiefly in China's literary writing, then we should not neglect Hu Shi's wide influence among Chinese intellectuals who strongly hoped that China would be engaged in the development of modernity. They both contributed a great deal to the origin and development of China's New Poetry up till the contemporary era.

During the period of the 1930s to the 1940s, and then during the 17 years before the Cultural Revolution, Whitman was still influential and favourably received among Chinese writers. Even after the Cultural Revolution, when modernism was largely translated and introduced into the Chinese context, the younger generation of writers enthusiastically read and talked about such high modernist writers as Joyce, Proust, Faulkner, Woolf and O'Neill, but they did not forget the pioneering role played by Walt Whitman. Among those young Chinese *Menglong* (Misty) poets, Gu Cheng was the most honest in admitting his indebtedness to Whitman.[15] Even in those poets of the post-*Menglong* period, we can still find the shadow of Whitman, both in aesthetic spirit and in poetic diction. And along with the publication of the two versions of Whitman's *Leaves of Grass*[16] and the deepening of the Whitman studies in China, Chinese scholars and intellectuals have fully recognized Whitman's anticipation of literary modernism in the West and his potential anticipation of China's modernity and modernist literary movement. Today, when we re-read Whitman from the modernist perspective in regard to his translation and reception in China, we cannot but conclude that this new reflection on the significance of Whitman and his poetry might well help to rewrite modern Chinese literary history from a new perspective.

TOWARD A NEW UNDERSTANDING OF WHITMAN IN A GLOBAL CONTEXT

When we discuss Whitman in the age of globalization, we cannot but think of the significance of Whitman and his literary creation in a global context. It is true that Whitman was a typical American poet and intellectual, uttering a sort of American voice characterized by American national and cultural identity. It is also true that Whitman produced all his poems in the nineteenth century when romanticism and then realism dominated writers' creative consciousness. But it is significant that many of his contemporaries have long gone out of fashion, and are seldom mentioned in the modern and postmodern periods, while Whitman is still observed not only in the English-speaking world but, along with the frequent cultural communication between the East and West recently, theoretically discussed in a global context. It must lead us to conclude that he belongs to the whole world, and transcends the artificial boundary between the East and West and the aesthetic gap between different literary movements. Since the beginning of the twentieth century, a large number of Western cultural trends and literary currents with their representative figures and works have been brought into China, exerting strong influences on Chinese literary creation and China's modernity, but few American writers or thinkers have affected both China's cultural modernity and literary modernist movement like Whitman. If I am asked to name some of the representatives, I would say that apart from Twain, Hemingway, Faulkner and Eliot in the twentieth century, Whitman is the only nineteenth-century American poet whose significance has even helped to form China's cultural project of modernity and rewrite modern Chinese literary history. In this sense, we can say that the profound study of Whitman has just begun in such a global context, for there are a lot of things for future Chinese scholars to do in the field of Whitman studies in a theoretical and comparative way.

11

Reconstructing Ibsen as an Artist: Translation and Reception of Ibsen in China

As one of the pioneering figures of literary modernism, Ibsen's remarkable contributions to the development of twentieth-century dramatic art have long been recognized, especially in the Western context. Although the sphere of elite literature and art is increasingly shrinking with the rise of popular culture and literature in the current age of globalization, Ibsen is still discussed theoretically both in the West and in the East.[1] I should point out, however, that Ibsen is largely appreciated in the Chinese context not as a dramatic artist, but rather as a revolutionary thinker of strong *avant-garde* consciousness and ideological tendency, especially his characterization of some of his rebellious women, such as Nora and Heddar Gabler, who have left such profound impressions on the Chinese audience, as well as drama scholars, that they have even forgotten that Ibsen is first of all an artist or, in its narrow sense, a dramatic artist. His significance in the formation of China's cultural modernity should not be denied, of course; as an artist, he has not only contributed to the rise of Chinese spoken drama in the twentieth century but has influenced large numbers of Chinese playwrights in their innovation of China's dramatic art. In this way, to study Ibsen as a thinker is somewhat misleading, especially in the contemporary era when people are so preoccupied with such Western thinkers as Nietzsche, Freud, Lacan, Foucault, Deleuze and Derrida that they seldom regard Ibsen as a thinker although he has indeed made some significant contributions to cultural modernity and literary modernism. As a thinker, Ibsen was overshadowed by these influential contemporary Western thinkers, such as Freud, who was once interested in Ibsen's work and was even inspired by him. For unlike all the above thinkers who have exerted great influence with their theoretic works, Ibsen has influenced and inspired Chinese intellectuals chiefly by his works of art. Thus, viewing the "real" Ibsen as an artist will pertinently evaluate his aesthetic significance in modern Chinese drama. The present chapter will call for a return to Ibsen's dramatic art by questioning his current inappropriate status in the Chinese context.

REFLECTIONS ON IBSEN AND MODERNITY IN THE CHINESE CONTEXT

In the development of Western and Chinese modernity, Henrik Ibsen as well as his drama has undoubtedly played an important and even irreplaceable role, which finds particular embodiment at the peak of European modernist literature and the May 4th period in China, with the latter strongly influenced by the former. Ibsen is thereby regarded chiefly as a great thinker and a very gifted and prophetic dramatic innovator, who, with his remarkable dramatic writing, has indeed influenced the development of modernity both in the West and in China.[2] It is true that in Western academic circles, scholars of different critical orientations have highly appreciated his artistic achievements or social and ideological impact. Some scholars highly praise him as the "greatest playwright since Shakespeare" or the "father of modern drama", simply because his works represent the very spirit of his time in a realistic manner, thus being of critical and realistic significance. Undoubtedly, Ibsen's criticism of social reality in his plays is so sharp that it has therefore much to do with the time he lived in as well as his strong personality which was obviously incompatible with the social conventions and critical environment then. This is probably one of the reasons why Ibsen was introduced in China chiefly as a master of critical realism. As the reception of Ibsen's drama was absolutely relevant to Chinese social realities as well as the cultural soil and receptive circumstances then, he was naturally classified under the tradition of nineteenth-century European realism. But according to the recent advances made in Western academic circles, Ibsen is discussed more as a modernist than a realist, for his appearance in the late nineteenth century actually heralded the rise of modernism in Western literature, and many of his prophetic and insightful ideas even paved the way for the development of modernity in both Western culture and thinking. Inspired by the advances made by my Western colleagues, I will re-explore Ibsen and his dramatic writing from the perspective of both cultural and aesthetic modernity, for to me, Ibsen should first of all be viewed as a literary master, or a dramatic artist, rather than a revolutionary thinker although he indeed stimulated Chinese intellectuals to rebel against social conventions and feudal and conservative ideologies. Many of the Chinese intellectuals and writers are so impressed by his dramatic characterization of such unforgettable characters as Nora, Heddar Gabler, Dr. Stockmann and Engstrand that they cannot but be influenced by Ibsen in their writing and critical practice. In order to pertinently evaluate Ibsen's contributions to modern Chinese drama, I will first reflect on the recent advances made in the Western context before associating them with the translation and reception of Ibsen's drama in China.

Analyzing Ibsen and his drama from the perspective of modernist theory is by no means a recent undertaking in Western academic circles. In one of my previous studies, I point out that the reason why Ibsen and his works are still favourably appreciated and studied by scholars is largely due to the fact that his plays are of more than one code, or multiple codes. That is, "apart from the realistic code, there are several other codes which are of course of critical value".[3] Through my careful observations, I can affirm that among other possible literary and cultural codes, modernism or modernity might well be one of the most important codes which makes his writings still relevant to the current theoretical debate about modernity and postmodernity.

Fredric Jameson, one of the most important scholars of modernity and postmodernity who has exerted a major influence on China's debate on the above issues, and inspired by the critical and creative reception of postmodernism in China, has recently redefined modernity by linking it to postmodernism.[4] To him, modernity cannot be significant without being associated with postmodernity. It is true that in his lifetime, Ibsen was incompatible with contemporary critical circles, partly due to his radical *avant-garde* outlook, and partly due to the visionary ideas inherent in his plays. Some of his plays which are frequently discussed today were not favourably received by audiences and critical circles during his lifetime. Among these plays are *Ghosts* and *An Enemy of the People*. When he published *Ghosts*, he was severely attacked by his contemporary critics. At the time, in the face of these attacks, Ibsen proudly declared, "All these fading and decrepit figures who have pounced on my play (*Ghosts*) will one day receive their crushing judgment in the literary histories of the future...My book belongs to the future."[5] It was certainly correct of him to write for the future. That is, his art is not a short-lived one, but rather one of eternal value and open for more interpretations in different ages. Like all the great literary masters, both in the West and in China, who might not have been considered important in their lifetimes, but who are now and then "rediscovered" by critics or scholars of the later generation, Ibsen's works largely point to the future readers although some of them were indeed well-received when he was still alive. Thus, his affirmation as mentioned above could not have been proved to be totally true in his lifetime, but with the passage of time, it is not difficult to find that many of the things he described a century ago still exist in the present age known as that of the postmodern, in which modernity to many people is not yet complete although it is being severely challenged by those who advocate postmodernity. So his affirmation has now been proved by the fact that some of his important plays are still performed on contemporary stages and continue to be favourably received by contemporary audiences both in the West and in China.[6]

When we discuss Ibsen in terms of modernity, we should first of all recognize that modernity in its broad and pluralistic sense should include both its cultural and political connotations as well as its aesthetic connotation. That is, it is viewed both as a literary and art spirit in its broadest artistic sense as well as a cultural project of enlightenment in its broadest cultural and intellectual sense. It is also true that in literature and art, different scholars may define modernism differently, but many of them view it chiefly as a European cultural and literary movement.[7] John Fletcher and James McFarlane, in discussing Ibsen's relationship with the modernist movement, pertinently suggest that there are two lines tracing the origin of the modernist literary movement: "... one substantive and thematic, the other formal and linguistic... On the one hand, there was the compulsive attention the eighties and nineties gave to the problematic and the contemporary; on the other, there was the restless exploration of the resources of prose as a dramatic medium. Both things point unwaveringly back to Ibsen."[8] Undoubtedly, the former definition is more Eurocentric, but the latter one given by Bradbury and McFarlane is more inclusive and characterized by advocating a sort of "boundless modernism", which has made a strong impact on the study of modernism in China. From their evident description, we can easily conclude that Ibsen really inspired many of the modernist writers, among whom are James Joyce and Samuel Beckett, the former even spending some time studying the Norwegian language for the sake of reading Ibsen directly. Thus, it is not strange that Ibsen is regarded as one of the pioneering figures of modernist literature more for artistic innovation than for ideology. Obviously, Bradbury and McFarlane, through scrutinizing Ibsen's dramatic texts, observe in his plays something different from realism and see the influence of Ibsen on the other modernist writers, thus correctly tracing all the inspiration back to Ibsen. In my view, the role played by Ibsen in the development of Western modernity manifests itself both in the field of cultural and intellectual enlightenment as well as that of literary innovation: His vivid portrayal of female characters anticipated the rise of the women's liberation movement in the 1960s, and his departure from traditional dramatic convention helped China's modern spoken drama to become mature and more appealing to the contemporary audience. That is perhaps the very reason why many of the writers who were once as well-known as Ibsen have now been forgotten while Ibsen still stands out from his era. I should say that Ibsen, among some other possible identities, is first and foremost a dramatist or an artist who has inspired and influenced people's minds chiefly by his dramatic art, for certain fashionable ideologies might well go out of fashion but the aesthetic and art spirit is eternal.

It is true that we now live in an age of globalization, in which modernist conventions are severely challenged. But why are Ibsen's plays still performed and why is he still being discussed by scholars from different parts of the world? When scholars of postmodern studies re-examine his works, they can easily read from his influence on the Theatre of Absurd—especially in *The Wild Duck* and other later works of his— some postmodern codes: His works never intend to answer the questions raised, thereby leaving it to the reader's imagination and interpretation to fill in the gaps. His plays themselves will never exhaust their meanings, but they are always open to reinterpretations from different angles. The ambivalence of his rhetoric, the multiple meanings of his symbolism and the uncertainty of his theme are all, to some extent, in tune with the postmodern spirit.[9] If a writer intends to have new significance discovered in his works in different ages, he should not just limit his theme to a particular time; he should deal with some fundamental problems that all human beings are confronted with. This is what Henrik Ibsen has done.

Speaking of Ibsen's plays as an organic whole with both realistic and modernist characteristics, Einar Haugen once insightfully pointed out that "each Ibsen play is a text that contains a hidden meaning, more or less consciously encoded in it by the author. Only by careful and penetrating study of the text will the reader be able to 'crack the code'."[10] Ibsen has therefore not only been revered as a great master of critical realism, but also—in the years during the rise of the modernist movement—as one of the major sources of literary modernism. Starting from Roman Jacobson's linguistic theory of communication, Haugen further symbolizes Ibsen's writing as good "for all seasons". To him, "as the world has changed, new issues have sprung up to engage the attention of the political, cultural, and theatrical world. Yet time and again someone finds that Ibsen has said something that is relevant to these issues and revives him, either on the stage or in new translations and adaptations."[11] The translations and adaptations of Ibsen's works in China have actually helped to create a new "Ibsen"—or "Ibsenism"—on the basis of Chinese readers' initiative understanding and creative construction.

Brian Johnston offers his own understanding and interpretation of Ibsen's works from a unique theoretical perspective different from the others. On the one hand, he does recognize the realistic dominant in Ibsen's play-writing and views his 12 later plays as a single realist cycle in which lies some deeper poetic intention; on the other hand, he intends to illustrate that "Ibsen's Realist Cycle is a universal battlefield in which one form after another of inadequate conceptions of reality— inadequate worlds—are defeated in combat with the absolute spirit".[12] As a matter of fact, by realism, he actually implies several codes, so Ibsen should be reinterpreted not just as a realistic writer. In Johnston's view, it is evident that the Ibsen "strategy" in his realist plays is two-fold. On the one hand, it shows the dialectical *subversion* of the nineteenth-century reality in the plays and, on the other hand, it represents the forced recovery of the archetypal from the past in a procedure similar to James Joyce's *Ulysses*, so his plays have actually encoded three forms of text: an ordinary text based on the linguistic structure of the writings themselves, a "supertext" of cultural reference for the author to constantly draw upon and, above all, an implied sub-text presented before the reader for him/her to read and analyze in a deconstructive way. To contemporary readers, it is easy to find that Ibsen's plays usually contain several contradictory elements—textuality, supertextuality, intertextuality and sub-textuality—which interact with and deconstruct one another, forming multiple codes in his dramatic texts and elements of uncertainty and intertextuality which find particular embodiment in the structure of his later plays, such as *The Wild Duck*, *Rosmersholm*, *The Lady from the Sea* and *When We Dead*

Awaken, which are frequently observed by Western scholars but seldom carefully discussed by Chinese scholars. That is one of the very reasons why most of China's Ibsen scholars could not engage in equitable dialogue with their international counterparts until recently, when several international conferences or seminars were held in Beijing and Shanghai in which China's younger generation of Ibsen scholars were able to directly communicate with their international counterparts.[13] To my mind, the above illustrates what we should describe as the "postmodern" codes, which has proved Lyotard's affirmation that those writings that appear later should not necessarily be postmodern, while those that appear earlier, such as Montaigne's essays, might well be postmodern.[14] This is just the postmodern paradox. Even in the future, scholars will further explore Ibsen's plays from new perspectives, and Ibsen will be subjected to continuous explorations and dynamic interpretations, both culturally and aesthetically, in the process of which some new significance might well be constructed and reconstructed largely through this sort of cultural translation.

IBSEN AND CHINA'S LITERARY MODERNITY: A REFLECTION

Compared to what has been achieved in Western academic circles, I should say rather frankly that Ibsen studies in China has been conducted in a very different orientation: He has been introduced and studied in China as a realist, or more exactly, a critical realist, with his plays depicting social problems inadequately highlighted and those of symbolism more or less neglected. Since realism in China, along with the theoretical debate on modernism and postmodernism, has been declining in importance in the past few decades, Ibsen is not frequently studied in the Chinese context although his plays are still popular and even occasionally staged in Beijing and Shanghai by some *avant-garde* directors. Although the mysterious and symbolic elements in his later plays are sometimes briefly mentioned, they are not profoundly analyzed. This must be quite relevant to the cultural and intellectual atmosphere at the time when Ibsen was first introduced in China. That was in the period of the significant May 4th Movement which marked not only the beginning of new Chinese literature but also the very beginning of Chinese cultural modernity. As is well-known, during that period, almost all the works of the Western literary masters were translated into Chinese and they profoundly influenced Chinese writing and the formation of Chinese literary and critical discourse. Ibsen was critically introduced in China—with his works being translated from English or German into Chinese—even earlier as the father of modern Western drama, but his influence found more embodiment not in dramatic innovation itself, but rather in intellectual and critical circles.[15]

Obviously, translation sometimes helps to reconstruct a canonical work of art or an artist in another cultural context in a misleading way. If we observe the critical and creative reception of Ibsen in China, we will probably find such a typical example. Before we call for a return to Ibsen as an artist, I think it is necessary to describe the characteristic features of Chinese modernity, or a metamorphosed version of Western modernity, to my Western colleagues as this is closely related to the role played by Ibsen. As is well-known, Chinese intellectuals in the first half of the twentieth century were most famous for "grabbism", in Lu Xun's terminology. That is, in order to fight against the feudal society and traditional cultural conventions, they would rather "grab" or "appropriate" foreign—or more exactly, Western—cultural and academic trends with which to attack the inflexible established Chinese cultural conventions. Thus, the construction of a sort of Chinese modernity became their important task. With respect to this controversial issue, Chinese men of letters and literary scholars respond or react in different ways and even argue among themselves, because quite a few of them always adopt a hostile attitude to the drastic change brought about during the May 4th period, nor are they satisfied with the radical change in Chinese literary tradition caused by the May 4th Movement. So what they want to do is to reverse the historical verdict of that significant cultural and literary event. But that is apparently impossible, for it was in the May 4th period that Chinese literature started its movement toward the world stage and gradually became part of world literature. Chinese literature, largely through the translation of various Western literary masters, began to step out of its isolated state and faced the impact from various foreign, especially Western, literary currents and cultural and academic trends. So it is not strange that today's scholars usually regard translated literature as being part of modern Chinese literature, which has actually formed a sort of "modern Chinese literary canon" different from the traditional Chinese literary convention as well as Western literature. Among all the translated Western masters, Ibsen stood out as one of the very few Western writers—if not the only one—whose literary achievements and ideological impact formed the basis of a special issue of the then influential intellectual journal, *Xin Qingnian* (New Youth).[16] Perhaps it is largely due to the strong and long-standing impact of this special issue on Ibsen that he has been viewed as a revolutionary thinker who anticipated the women's liberation movement in China. A sort of "Ibsenism" of Chinese characteristics was thus born on the Chinese cultural soil. If we do not disagree with the idea that translated literature is part of modern Chinese literature, then we should also recognize that "Ibsenism" in the Chinese context is actually a translated or constructed concept, largely for the purpose of attacking the evil Chinese reality and the feudal social and cultural conventions. It serves more of a pragmatic function than it is of aesthetic significance. So to my mind, it is absolutely necessary to deal with Ibsen's artistic achievements now. Viewing him only as a revolutionary thinker is far from enough since he was first of all an *avant-garde* artist who not only wrote for his contemporaries but, more importantly, for his future audiences. That is one of the reasons why we still discuss Ibsen in today's Chinese context after his death nearly a hundred years ago. He is not only closely related to China's political and cultural modernity, but also more profoundly stimulating to China's men of letters and theatrical artists.

As far as Chinese modernity is concerned, I will describe the characteristics that are different from what appeared in the Western cultural context. Since Chinese intellectuals are famous for "grabbism", they grab everything from abroad for their own use, which finds particular embodiment in the significant May 4th period when almost all the Western trends of culture and literary thought were translated, introduced and metamorphosed in the Chinese context; dealing with modern Chinese literature from the comparative perspective of influence–reception studies is an important strategy in rewriting modern Chinese literary history.[17] First of all, we should admit that even if Chinese modernity exists, it is still something translated and introduced from the West although it represents, to a large extent, the internal logic of the development of modern Chinese culture and thinking. Thus, like the modernity in other regions, Chinese modernity, as part of the global trend of modernity, is characterized by its totality and exclusiveness. It is closely related to the Chinese people's cause of liberation and therefore very functional and enlightenment-oriented. Thus, it is easy for Chinese intellectuals to accept Ibsen as their spiritual leader since many of his plays do offer sharp critiques of human and social evils. But on the other hand, we should not forget that the effect of the enlightenment of literature is first of all realized by means of an aesthetic rather than an ideological purpose. People can only get ideological inspiration and aesthetic pleasure through reading works of art or watching the performance of the plays. Since Ibsen was chiefly a playwright, his enlightenment role was largely played by his dramatic art. In this respect, we should show a pertinent appreciation of Ibsen's contributions to Chinese spoken drama, which is undoubtedly a product of Chinese–Western cultural communication and interaction. Under the influence of and inspired by Ibsen and his dramas, there appeared a few masters of Chinese drama in the first half of Chinese literary history: Cao Yu, Hong Shen, Ouyang Yuqian and some others created quite a few unforgettable plays of the Ibsen type, and a few Ibsen-type characters appeared in their dramatic texts. So Ibsen in China was certainly "metamorphosed", or, as I have just pointed out, "constructed". He was dynamically "translated" into the Chinese context and produced some new significance for Chinese intellectuals and artists. The same is true of his major character Nora, with many "Noras" of Chinese characteristics appearing both on the screen and on stage. Since Ibsen has become a modern Western canon open to different interpretations or reinterpretations, and different constructions or reconstructions, and since different Ibsen scholars have constructed different "Ibsens" in different cultural contexts, including the Chinese context, why shouldn't we Chinese scholars offer our own reconstruction of Ibsen in regard to the critical and creative reception of his dramas in the Chinese context? That is the very point I will address in the concluding section of this chapter.

TOWARD A CONSTRUCTION OF IBSENIZATION

So far, I have deconstructed some misleading concepts about Ibsen in China. People might well raise the question: What is your theoretical construction since great writers are always open to future interpretations and criticisms? That is what I will try to do in this short concluding section. Here—inspired by Marx and Engels who, in their close reading of Shakespeare's dramatic works, constructed from the aesthetic perspective a sort of Shakespeareanization largely on the basis of his great artistic achievements—I would like to offer my own theoretical and aesthetic construction, or Ibsenization. This is perhaps my tentative strategy to call for a "return to Ibsen as an artist". As we know, Ibsen's achievements have been theoretically studied and ideologically constructed as a sort of Ibsenism by Brandes and George Bernard Shaw in the Western context, and then by Hu Shi and some other May 4th writers and intellectuals in the Chinese context. It is without a doubt that such an Ibsenism has contributed a great deal to the development of cultural and political modernity both in the West and in China. What the above critics emphasize are not his aesthetic achievements but rather his strong personality, characterized by his individualism and his sharp critique of various social problems. It is certainly understandable for them to do so in their time when literature was largely used to expose and criticize social evils and educate ordinary people so that they would be enlightened through reading literary works. But literature also has its unique function which cannot be replaced by any other ideological doctrine although it has certain ideological tendencies. That is, its aesthetic function and artistic appeal are attractive to the broad reading public. Obviously, I do not want to deny the critics' emphasis on the ideological and enlightening role played by Ibsen in the development of modernity, nor do I want to overlook the significant constructions and their consequent impact on the promotion of China's political and cultural modernity in history. What I intend to propose here is simply a "return to the real Ibsen as an artist" and an "aesthetic turn" in China's Ibsen studies since we have focused too much on his enlightening function rather than his artistic achievements. In this way, China's Ibsen scholars will be able to engage in equitable and direct dialogue with the international Ibsen scholarship on the basis of this perspective.[18]

If we recognize that Shakespeare's works capture the very spirit of the Renaissance period and represent the perfect combination of realism and romanticism, then it is logical to conclude that Ibsen's works, especially his later works, exactly capture the spirit of the *fin de siècle* and represent the perfect combination of modernism and avant-gardism, with some of his later plays even open for poststructuralist interpretations. If we try to point out that Shakespeareanization is chiefly defined by Shakespeare's superb characterization—with his major characters being fully developed—then we have full reason to argue that Ibsen has also created a group of female characters who are both unforgettable and who hold great appeal for the twentieth-century audience. If we recognize that Shakespeare's ideological tendency is not directly expressed as is Schiller's, then I would argue that many of Ibsen's ideological insights are communicated symbolically rather than literally. Obviously, we have constructed various literary and aesthetic concepts, including Shakespeareanization and Ibsenization, but we need a more profound theoretic elaboration of these concepts. As for the theoretical concept I have constructed in this chapter, I will elaborate it elsewhere in detail. Here, I just hold that we still have a long way to go in exploring Ibsen as an artist and studying his aesthetic achievements rather than merely viewing him as a revolutionary thinker or a critical realist and his works as the quintessence of Ibsenism.

Notes

CHAPTER 1 – GLOBALIZATION AND CULTURE: THE CHINESE CULTURAL AND INTELLECTUAL STRATEGY

1   Cf. William J. Martin, *The Global Information Society* (Hampshire: Aslib Gower, 1995), 11–12.

2   Michael Hardt and Antonio Negri, preface to *Empire* (Cambridge, Massachusetts: Harvard University Press, 2000), xv.

3   Cf. Roland Robertson, *Globalization: Social Theory and Global Culture* (London: Sage, 1992), 100.

4   Fredric Jameson, "Notes on Globalization as a Philosophical Issue", in *The Cultures of Globalization*, eds. Fredric Jameson and Masao Miyoshi (Durham, NC: Duke University Press, 1998), 73.

5   Karl Marx and Frederick Engels, *The Communist Manifesto* (Boston and New York: Bedford/St. Martin's, 1999), 69.

6   Cf. Fredric Jameson and Masao Miyoshi, eds., *The Cultures of Globalization* (Durham, NC: Duke University Press, 1998), 55.

7   It is a good beginning that a journal called *Wenhua yanjiu: Xifang yu zhongguo* (Cultural Studies: West and China) has been published twice a year by Tianjin Social Sciences Publishing House since the summer of 2000, which will not only introduce to the Chinese scholars the most recent advances made in Western cultural studies but provide theoretical analysis of contemporary Chinese cultural phenomena, especially those concerned with the social community and the media's effect on people's lives and the cultural market.

8   Leslie Fiedler, *Cross the Border, Close the Gap* (New York: Stein and Day, 1972), 80.

9   There was a heated debate on the issue of the crisis of the humanistic spirit in 1995–1996, launched by a group of scholars in Shanghai round the journals of *Shanghai wenxue* (Shanghai Literature) and *Dushu* (Reading). Dissatisfied with the rise of popular culture and the prevalence of postmodern theory in academic circles, these scholars tried to recover the old tradition of humanistic spirit, something similar to a new humanism. But this debate came to an end without any result.

10 It is true that some Chinese scholars who are very familiar with the most recent advances made in Western academic and theoretical studies have realized the importance of reconstructing Chinese culture in the age of globalization. In this respect, the Symposium on Globalization and the Construction of Chinese Culture (Beijing, September 1999) has made a remarkable start. What should be particularly mentioned here is that at the symposium, two eminent Western scholars in the field of globalization, Arif Dirlik and Gabrielle Schwab, were invited to make keynote speeches and engage in direct dialogues with Chinese scholars.

11   Cf. *New Literary History* 28, no. 1 (1997), especially those essays by Terry Eagleton, Wang Ning, Liu Kang, Sheldon Lu, Wang Fengzhen and Jonathan Arac.

12   This journal, published as a book series, is co-edited by Tao Dongfeng, Jin Yuanpu and Gao Bingzhong and its first three issues were published by the Publishing House of Tianjin Academy of Social Sciences. But due to the financial problems of the publishing house, the fourth issue was published by Central Compilation and Translation Press in Beijing in 2003.

13   As for an ideal dialogic, rather than oppositional, relationship between comparative literature and cultural studies, cf. Wang Ning, "Confronting Globalization: Cultural Studies versus Comparative Literature Studies?" *Neohelicon* 28 (2001): 1, 55–66.

14   Cf. Arif Dirlik, *Hou geming fenwei* (*The Post-Revolutionary Aura*), trans. Wang Ning et al. (Beijing: China Social Sciences Publishing House, 1999). This book is a selection of Dirlik's essays, published first in English in the West and then in Chinese in China, which is frequently quoted by Chinese scholars in their study of globalization and postcolonialism. The second selection of his essays, *Kuaguo ziben shidai de houzhimin piping* (*Postcolonial Criticism in an Age of Transnational Capitalization*), edited and chiefly translated by Wang Ning, has been published by Peking University Press in 2004.

15   Arif Dirlik, "The Global in the Local", in *Global/Local: Cultural Production and the Transnational Imaginary*, eds. Rob Wilson and Wimal Disanayake (Durham and London: Duke University Press, 1996), 35.

16   Cf. Arif Dirlik, "Culture Against History? The 'West' in the Search for an East Asian Identity" (keynote speech delivered at the Symposium on Globalization and the Construction of Chinese Culture, Beijing, China, 25 September 1999).

17   This can be easily seen in the grand commemoration of the 2550th anniversary of the birth of Confucius in Beijing and Shandong, his native birthplace.

18   A recent good symbol is that the authoritative *Wenyi bao* (Literature and Art Gazette) has published some essays discussing the issue of cultural industry or cultural production in the context of globalization since March 1998.

19   Jameson offered this insightful idea in his remarks about my lecture on Chinese postmodernity at Duke University on 18 October 1996, which has certainly given me some revelations.

20   Fredric Jameson, *Postmodernism or the Cultural Logic of Late Capitalism* (Durham: Duke University Press, 1991), 31.

21   Apart from Jameson's influence, those Chinese critics advocating Third World culture and localism are Zhang Yiwu, Wang Yichuan, Zhang Fa and Wang Gan. See some of their essays published in *Wenyi zhengming* (Debate on Literature and Art) and *Zhongshan* (Purple Mountains) in recent years.

22   In a recent interview with Zhang Xudong, Jameson, in discussing such important issues as the historicity of theory, Marxism and late capitalism,

dialectical thinking and cultural studies and locality, refers to the Chinese intellectual situation now and then. See Xudong Zhang, "Marxism and the Historicity of Theory: An Interview with Fredric Jameson", *New Literary History* 29, no. 3 (1998): 353–383.

23   Cf. Michael Sprinker, ed., *Edward Said: A Critical Reader* (Oxford, UK: Blackwell, 1992), 255.

24   Perhaps September 11 has served as a starting point for changing the almost oppositional relations between China and the United States, with President Bush's recent visit to China as the culminating positive result.

25   As for the change of literary and cultural dominance from that of the New Period to that of the Post-New Period in current China, cf. Wang Ning, "From Psychoanalysis to Schizoanalysis: Reflections on Current Chinese Literary Cultures", *Social Semiotics* 7, no. 3 (1997): 323–334.

26   Along with China's success in bidding for the Olympic Games in the year 2008, more and more Chinese people have realized the importance of communicating with the outside world in English. And more and more scholars have realized the importance of publishing in international journals in English.

CHAPTER 2 – GLOBALIZATION, CULTURAL STUDIES AND TRANSLATION STUDIES

1   At the 15th Triennial Congress of the International Comparative Literature Association (Leiden, 1997), the topic of the seventh session was "Reconstructing Cultural Memory: Translation, Scripts, Literacy", and almost all the papers read in this session dealt with translation from the cultural perspective.

2   Ironically, there was no independent department of translation in all of China's universities in the mainland previously, except for one college training translators for the United Nations at Beijing Foreign Studies University, while in Hong Kong, at least two or more universities—the Chinese University of Hong Kong and Lingnan University—have their own departments of translation. This must be associated with the long-marginalized position of translation in China's university curriculum. Fortunately, due to the joint efforts made by China's translation and culture scholars, several departments or schools of translation have been established in some universities like Shanghai International Studies University and Guangdong University of Foreign Studies.

3   This finds particular embodiment in China's institutionalization of translation studies at the graduate level for the MA programme in some universities. Internationally, the Chinese Translators Association also has close contacts with the International Federation of Translators.

4   Since the beginning of the 1980s, quite a few Chinese scholars have published in such international journals of translation studies as *Target*, *Perspectives* and *Babel*, which is indeed remarkable among all the fields of social sciences and the humanities. What is even more exciting is that since 2003, the international journal, *Perspectives: Studies in Translatology*,

has been co-sponsored by the University of Copenhagen and Tsinghua University, and it is also published yearly in China by Tsinghua University Press.

5   Cf. Eugene Eoyang Chen, *The Transparent Eye: Reflections on Translation, Chinese Literature, and Comparative Poetics* (Honolulu: University of Hawaii Press, 1993), 3.

6   Edward Said, *Orientalism* (New York: Vintage Books, 1979), 1.

7   *Ibid.*, 21–22.

8   As for the binary opposition between Orientalism and Occidentalism and its deconstruction, cf. Wang Ning, "Orientalism versus Occidentalism?" *New Literary History* 28, no. 1 (1997): 57–67.

9   I should point out here that even today, translation studies does not have an independent MA programme in China's universities although there have been some MA programmes for translation studies in the past few years. Due to the recent readjustment of disciplines, it is included in the programme for foreign linguistics and applied linguistics. MA students or PhD students in translation studies are also enrolled in some programmes on comparative literature and world literature,.

10   As for the critique of postcolonial theory in regard to the decolonization of Chinese culture, cf. Wang Ning, "Postcolonial Theory and the 'Decolonization' of Chinese Culture", *ARIEL* 28, no. 4 (1997): 33–47.

11   *Ibid.*, 44–45.

CHAPTER 3 – GLOBALIZING CHINESE LITERATURE: TOWARD A REWRITING OF CONTEMPORARY CHINESE LITERARY CULTURE

1   In this respect, the International Conference on Globalization and the Future of the Humanities held in Beijing on 17–20 August 1998 offered a good occasion on which scholars from the West and the East got together to discuss what globalization has brought to the humanities and social sciences. See the special issue of essays selected from the conference papers in *Social Semiotics* 10, no. 2 (2000); and Wang Ning and Xue Xiaoyuan, eds., *Quanqiuhua yu houzhimin piping* (Globalization and Postcolonial Criticism) (Beijing: Central Compilation and Translation Press, 1998).

2   "*Petites histoires*" here refers to those works written by some contemporary writers in a parodic way based on the historical records of certain famous or notorious historical figures, such as Empress Wu (Wu Zetian), Emperor Kangxi (Kangxi dadi) and Cao Cao. These "new historical" writings are so popular in the book market that they have even occupied the original canonical literary market.

3   During my lecture tour in Stockholm, I interviewed Professor Kjell Espmark, a member of the Swedish Academy and Chairman of its Nobel Prize Committee, who also holds the same opinion as I do and who is very confident about the future of literature.

4   Harold Bloom, "The Dialectics of Literary Tradition", in *Early Postmodernism: Foundational Essays*, ed. Paul Bove (Durham, NC: Duke University Press, 1995), 173–174.

5   As for the detailed description of the influence of Western theories and cultural trends on Chinese literature of the twentieth century, see Yue Daiyun and Wang Ning, eds., *Xifang wenyisichao yu ershishiji zhongguo wenxue* (Western Trends of Literary Thought and Twentieth-Century Chinese Literature) (Beijing: China Social Sciences Publishing House, 1990).

6   As far as the start of globalization is concerned, I always think that it started long ago as a process before the twentieth century, cf. Wang Ning, "Globalization and Culture: The Chinese Cultural and Intellectual Strategy", *Neohelicon* XXIX, no. 2 (2002), 103–116. Also, to Roland Robertson, the globalization in culture started even before the discovery of the Americas. Cf. Roland Robertson, "Globality: Mainly a Western View" (keynote speech delivered at the Forum on Globalization and Culture, Tsinghua University, China, 25 November 2001). Also cf. Roland Robertson and Kathleen E. White, eds., *Globalization: Critical Concepts*, vols. I–VI (London & New York: Routledge, 2003).

7   As for the different evaluations about the May 4th Movement made by overseas scholars, see Chow Tse-tsung, *The May Fourth Movement: Intellectual Revolution in Modern China* (Cambridge, Massachusetts: Harvard University Press, 1960), 338–355.

8   Cf. Wang Yuanhua, "Wei wusi jingshen yi bian" ("A Defence of the May 4th Spirit"), in *Wusi: duoyuan de fansi* (The May 4th Movement: Pluralistic Reflections), eds. Lin Yusheng et al. (Hong Kong: Sanlian Press, 1989), 1. Also worth reading are some essays in the book criticizing Wang's idea.

9   Please refer to those essays in the above book in which different opinions from Wang Yuanhua's are offered.

10   Lu Xun, "Wo zenme zuoqi xiaoshuo lai" ("How I Started to Write Novels"), in *Lu Xun quanji* (Collected Works of Lu Xun), vol. 4 (Beijing: People's Literature Press, 1989), 512.

11   As for the different cultural dominants between New Period literature and Post-New Period literature, see Wang Ning, "Hou xinshiqi: yizhong lilun miaoshu" ("Post-New Period: A Theoretical Description"), *Huacheng*, no. 3 (1995); and "From Psychoanalysis to Schizoanalysis: Reflections on Current Chinese Literary Cultures", *Social Semiotics* 7, no. 3 (1997): 323–334.

12   If we say that the postmodernism debate started with the critique or construction of postmodernism by Irving Howe, Susan Sontag, Leslie Fiedler and Ihab Hassan in North American cultural and critical circles, then its entry into European intellectual circles was marked by Jean-Francois Lyotard's book, *La Condition postmoderne: Rapport sur la savoir*, in 1979.

13. As for this, the relationship between Chinese literature of the New Period and that of the Post-New Period is very similar to the relationship between modernist literature and postmodernist literature in the Western context. Hence, it will be misleading just to view the term "Post-New Period" as a

term of chronological periodization, for some insightful overseas Chinese scholars and sinologists have long recognized the sign of such a "transition" in the late 1980s in China.

14   In this aspect, cf. the forum presided over by Chen Xiaoming et al., "Houxiandai wenhua de kuozhang he cuowei" ("The Expansion and Paradox of Postmodern Culture"), *Shanghai wenxue* (Shanghai Literature), no. 3 (1994): 62–69. In this piece, the "postmodern" concept and "postmodernism" discussed by them are coloured more with a sort of localism, and are more or less different from the original meaning of these terms in the Western context.

15   Perhaps this is one of the reasons why sinological studies in these countries or regions have a long tradition and have been developing rapidly in recent years.

16   J. Hillis Miller, "Will Comparative Literature Survive the Globalization of the University and the New Regime of Telecommunications?" *Tamkang Review* XXXI, no. 1 (Autumn 2000): 13.

17   Samuel Huntington, "The Clash of Civilizations?" *Foreign Affairs* 72, no. 3 (Summer 1993), in *A Foreign Affairs Reader* (1993): 22–49. When the article was first published, it aroused great debates among Arabs and Chinese for its radical affirmation.

18   In the volumes *International Postmodernism: Theory and Literary Practice* (Amsterdam/Philadelphia: John Benjamins Publishing Co., 1997) and *Romanticist Prose and Fiction* (forthcoming) of the series *The Comparative History of Literature in European Languages* to which I have contributed a chapter, there are descriptions dealing with the reception of each of these literary currents in China.

19   Cf. Ralph Cohen, ed., introduction to *The Future of Literary Theory* (London and New York: Routledge, 1989), vii–viii.

20   In this respect, some American sinologists, such as Kang-i Sun Chang, are trying to reinterpret classical Chinese literary works from the perspective of a Western theory in an attempt to reconstruct the literary canon. This trend should attract our attention.

21   Harold Bloom, *The Western Canon: The Books and the School of the Ages* (New York: Harcourt Brace Company, 1994), 17.

22   *Ibid.*, 20.

23   In this respect, see Zhu Dake et al., *Shi zuojia pipan shu* (Critiques of Ten Well-Known Chinese Writers) (Xi'an: Shanxi Normal University Press, 1999).

CHAPTER 4 – THE POPULARIZATION OF ENGLISH AND THE "DECOLONIZATION" OF CHINESE CRITICAL DISCOURSE

1   This finds particular embodiment in the recent fad of Chinese studies (*guoxue*), which is obviously a postcolonial strategy set up to oppose Western influence on Chinese culture and academic studies.

2   In this respect, the authoritative *Wenyi bao* (Literature and Art Gazette) launched a discussion in late 1998 on the cultural industry and cultural studies. Those who are opposed to cultural studies are usually scholars of English literature before the contemporary era, as the dominance of cultural studies has made it difficult for them to get published.

3   Some Chinese journals of literary studies, especially the authoritative *Wenyi yanjiu* (Literature and Art Studies), adopt a pluralistic attitude toward the new cultural and academic trends, such as postmodernism, postcolonialism and, recently, cultural studies. See especially articles by Wang Ning, Zhang Yiwu, Tao Dongfeng, and Yang Naiqiao in the issues of the journal between 1997 and 2003.

4   Since 1995, cultural studies has been discussed extensively in some major critical and learned journals. In August 1995, the International Conference on Cultural Studies: China and the West held in Dalian was co-sponsored by Peking University and the University of Virginia. As a result, a special issue (on the basis of selected conference papers) of the leading journal *New Literary History* 28, no. 1 (1997) was published. Also, eight papers were published in Chinese in *Guowai wenxue* (Foreign Literatures), no. 2 (1996).

5   As for Bhabha's influence in China, his first visit to China and his lectures at Tsinghua University on 25–26 June 2002 have certainly promoted it.

6   For instance, at the moment, China's modernizing process is actually mixed up with a sort of postmodernity, which manifests itself in those advanced special economic zones, such as Shenzhen and Zhuhai, while in the broad rural areas and small cities, its modernizing process is still composed of certain premodern elements.

7   It is true that due to their refusal to take the English examination, some researchers' promotions in the Chinese Academy of Social Sciences were delayed even though they obtained their PhDs in Western universities.

8   In this respect, Cao Shunqing is representative. See Cao Shunqing, "Wenlun shiyuzheng yu wenhua bingtai" ("Lacking in Discourse in Literary Criticism and Cultural Sickness"), *Wenyi zhengming* (Debate on Literature and Art), no. 2 (1996): 50–58.

9   Actually, the idea of setting up a "Chinese School" of comparative literature was first put forward by the comparatists overseas (and in Taiwan), such as John Deeney and Chen Peng-hsiang in the 1970s. In the 1980s, when comparative literature was introduced into China's mainland, this idea was once popular and attractive. Now this issue has been raised again by Cao Shunqing and others, but it has become less attractive in the broad context of cultural studies and globalization.

10   For instance, at the Sixth Triennial Congress of the Chinese Comparative Literature Association (1999), there was a session exclusively dealing with the issue of a "Chinese School" in comparative literature studies.

11   In encouraging Chinese scholars of the humanities and social sciences to write in English and publish in prestigious international journals, I have, on several occasions, given lectures introducing and commenting on these journals in quite a few Chinese universities. Cf. Wang Ning, "Guoji yingwen quanwei xueshu qikan pingjie ji xiezuo celue" ("Introduction to

Some Prestigious International Learned Journals and the Writing Techniques"), *Zhongguo yanjiusheng* (Chinese Graduate Students), no. 5 (2003): 17–21.

12   To fill this gap in China's comparative literature studies, Ji Xianlin and I have edited a series on Chinese culture in the West, which includes seven books dealing with the influence of Chinese culture on, and its dissemination in, Europe and North America. It is published by Hebei People's Press (1998).

13   Cf. Wang Ning, "Postcolonial Theory and the 'Decolonization' of Chinese Culture", *ARIEL* 28, no. 4 (1997): 33–47.

14   Indeed, it was not until the beginning of the 1980s when the sinologist Goran Malmqvist became a member of the Swedish Academy and the Nobel Committee that the Committee had a member who understood the Chinese language.

15   The indication is that more and more self-supported schools for teaching Chinese to foreigners have appeared in Beijing and other Chinese cities.

16   Actually, not only have ordinary students of Chinese studies in the West realized the fact that reading Chinese literature in its English translation is a less rewarding experience as certain elements are lost in the translation, but some distinguished Western scholars have also come to this conclusion. For instance, at the Forum on Globalization and Literary Studies held on 4 September 2003, J. Hillis Miller said publicly, "If I were twenty years younger, I would start to learn the Chinese language."

CHAPTER 5 – TRANSLATOLOGY: TOWARD A SCIENTIFIC DISCIPLINE

1   See Eugene Nida, *Towards a Science of Translating, with Special Reference to Principles and Procedures Involved in Bible Translating* (Leiden: Adler's Foreign Books, 1964), 159.

2   Lawrence Venuti, "'Introduction' to Derrida's 'What is a "Relevant" Translation?'" *Critical Inquiry* 27, no. 2 (Winter 2001): 170.

3   Jacques Derrida, "What is a 'Relevant' Translation?" *Critical Inquiry* 27, no. 2 (Winter 2001): 175.

4   Lawrence Venuti, "'Introduction' to Derrida's 'What is a "Relevant" Translation?'" *Critical Inquiry* 27, no. 2 (Winter 2001): 172.

5   Jacques Derrida, "What is a 'Relevant' Translation?" *Critical Inquiry* 27, no. 2 (Winter 2001): 177.

6   *Ibid.*, 182.

7   As for my preliminary definition of translation, cf. Wang Ning, "Globalization, Cultural Studies and Translation Studies", *Translation Quarterly*, no. 15 (2000): 37–50.

8   J. William Martin, *The Global Information Society* (Hampshire: Aslib Gower, 1995), 11–12.

9   Roland Robertson, *Globalization: Social Theory and Global Culture* (London: Sage, 1992), 100.

10   See Fredric Jameson, "Notes on Globalization as a Philosophical Issue", in *The Cultures of Globalization*, eds. Fredric Jameson and Masao Miyoshi (Durham, NC: Duke University Press, 1998), 55–58.

11   Gayati Chakrovorty Spivak, *A Critique of Postcolonial Reason: Toward a History of the Vanishing Present* (Cambridge, Massachusetts: Harvard University Press, 1999), 155.

12   Lawrence Venuti, "'Introduction' to Derrida's 'What is a "Relevant" Translation?'" *Critical Inquiry* 27, no. 2 (Winter 2001): 169.

13   Cf. Roman Jakobson, "On Linguistic Aspects of Translation", in *On Translation*, ed. Reuben Brower (Cambridge, Massachusetts: Harvard University Press, 1959), 232–239.

14   Walter Benjamin, "The Task of the Translator", in *Illuminations*, trans. Harry Zohn, ed. Hannah Arendt (New York: Harcourt Brace and World, 1968), 69.

CHAPTER 6 – TRANSLATION STUDIES IN THE CONTEXT OF CHINESE-WESTERN COMPARATIVE CULTURE STUDIES

1   Here, I would like to show a contemporary example. That is, of all the contemporary young Chinese writers, many have been influenced by Western literature—or more exactly, by (translated) Western literature—especially in language, rather than by classical Chinese literature. One of the typical contemporary Chinese *avant-garde* novelists is Yu Hua, who openly affirms, "When writers like our generation began to write, we were most indebted to translated novels rather than classical Chinese literature, let alone modern Chinese literature. I have always been thinking that the contributions made to the construction and development of new Chinese language should be first of all attributed to those translators, who have found an intermediary way of expression between the Chinese language and foreign languages..." See *Zuojia* (Writers), no. 3 (1996): 6.

2   In present-day China, there are quite a few journals on foreign language teaching and research or foreign literature studies, in which some essays on translation studies are published now and then, but there is only one journal sponsored by the Chinese Translators Association—that is, *Zhongguo fanyi* (China Translators)—in which one can hardly find any theoretical or academic articles on substantial translation studies done in the past, let alone other journals.

3   Here, I should remind my readers that even to my students at the undergraduate level, such binary opposition holds true for both sides, for I always come across such affirmative evaluation in the students' papers since I started teaching the course, "Translation from Chinese into English: Theory and Practice", at my university.

4 See Eugene Nida, and Charles R. Taber, *The Theory and Practice of Translation* (Leiden: Brill, 1969), 12.

5 André Lefevere, *Translating Literature: Practice and Theory in a Comparative Literature Context* (New York: Modern Language Association, 1992), 6.

6 As for Western influence on modern and contemporary Chinese literature, see especially Wang Ning, "Confronting Western Influence: Rethinking Chinese Literature of the New Period", *New Literary History* 24, no. 4 (1993): 905–926.

7 Fred Inglis, *Cultural Studies* (Oxford, UK: Blackwell, 1993), 85.

8 One of the typical examples is Lu Xun's controversial essay entitled "Ying yi yu wen xue de jiejixing" ("Literal Translation and the Nature of Class Struggle"), which aroused heated debates among the men of letters in the 1930s.

9 Cf. Wang Zuoliang, *Fanyi: sikao yu shibi* (Translation: Experiments and Reflections) (Beijing: Foreign Languages Teaching and Research Press, 1989), 35.

10 This quotation is taken from James Hightower's book, *The Poetry of Tao Ch'ien* (Oxford: Clarendon Press, 1970).

CHAPTER 7 – TRANSLATING THEORY: TOWARD A RECONSTRUCTION OF CHINESE CRITICAL DISCOURSE

1 Rainer Schulte and John Biguenet, eds., introduction to *Theories of Translation: An Anthology of Essays from Dryden to Derrida* (Chicago and London: University of Chicago Press, 1992), 9.

2 In this respect, we should refer particularly to Homi Bhabha's article, "How Newness Enters the World: Postmodern Space, Postcolonial Times and the Trials of Cultural Translation," in his *The Location of Culture* (London and New York: Routledge, 1994), 212–235.

3 Eugene Nida, *Towards a Science of Translating, with Special Reference to Principles and Procedures Involved in Bible Translating* (Leiden: Adler's Foreign Books, 1964), 159.

4 As far as Lin Shu's contribution to the construction of Chinese modernity is concerned, cf. Wang Ning, "Xiandaixing, fanyi wenxue yu zhongguo xiandai wenxue jingdian chonggou" ("Modernity, Translated Literature and the Reconstruction of Modern Chinese Literary Canon"), *Wenyi yanjiu* (Literature and Art Studies), no. 6 (2002).

5 Terry Eagleton, "Shakespeare and the Letter of the Law", in *The Eagleton Reader*, ed. Stephen Regan (Oxford: Blackwell, 1998), 72.

6 Rainer Schulte and John Biguenet, eds., introduction to *Theories of Translation: An Anthology of Essays from Dryden to Derrida* (Chicago and London: University of Chicago Press, 1992), 8.

7 Although these literary masters did not do much theoretical translation, they did introduce or comment on their translated Western writers from their own theoretical perspectives.

8   I will give a few examples of the translation of literary works and theoretic works from languages other than their original languages: Some of Marx's works were translated either from Japanese or from Russian, Ibsen's plays were translated mostly from English and German, and Freud's works were translated mostly from English, etc.

9   According to the current division of academic disciplines made by the Chinese State Council Degree Committee, translation studies is included under the discipline of foreign linguistics and applied linguistics although it used to be an independent discipline. But some Chinese scholars of translation studies are still trying to "demarginalize" this "repressed" sub-discipline in an attempt to highlight it as an independent discipline parallel with that of foreign linguistics and applied linguistics.

10   Interestingly enough, after the enthusiastic introduction and translation of Western postmodern theories and cultural trends, some Chinese scholars in turn came to reflect on the question of modernity, which found particular embodiment in the "Habermas fad" in China, when he conducted a short lecture tour in Beijing in April 2001.

11   Gayatri Chakrovorty Spivak, *A Critique of Postcolonial Reason: Toward a History of the Vanishing Present* (Cambridge, Massachusetts: Harvard University Press, 1999), 64.

12   See the advertising phrase printed on the back cover of Spivak's recently published book, *A Critique of Postcolonial Reason*.

13   At my invitation, Homi Bhabha visited China and gave a keynote speech entitled "The Black Savant and the Dark Princess" at the Tsinghua–Harvard Advanced Forum on Postcolonialism on 25 June 2002 in Beijing, in which he stated that, on the one hand, there is the project of globalization, but on the other hand, there is the process of "minoritization, which might be another type of globalization". Since his speech was translated and the Chinese version published in the leading Chinese literary journal, *Wenxue pinglun* (Literary Review, no. 6, 2006), it has given Chinese scholars of literary and cultural studies quite some inspiration.

14   One of the most recent examples in this respect is the huge success of Ang Lee's film, *Wohu canglong* (*Crouching Tiger, Hidden Dragon*), in the international cultural market and film industry although it has aroused some controversy among mainland Chinese audiences.

15   Although in the past, Chinese scholars of translation studies liked to debate about the three principles of "*xin* (faithfulness), *da* (expressiveness) and *ya* (elegance)" formulated by Yan Fu, they have now realized the importance of communicating with the international scholarship. They not only publish extensively in such international journals of translation studies as *Perspectives*, *Target*, *META* and *Babel*, but also actively involve themselves in the Asian Translators' Forum and other international conferences on translation studies.

16   In this respect, I should mention the fact that due to their editors' far-sightedness and cross-cultural perspectives, such international journals as *Perspectives: Studies in Translatology*, *META*, *Target* and *Babel* have published numerous articles written in English by Chinese scholars, thus making the international circle of translation studies aware of the state of the art

of translation studies in China. *Perspectives* (1996 and 2003) and *META* (1997) have even put out special issues on Chinese translation studies.

17   Katerina Clark and Michael Holquist, *Mikhail Bakhtin* (Cambridge, Massachusetts: Harvard University Press, 1984), vii.

18   *Bahejin quanji* (Collected Works of Mikhail Bakhtin) was published in Chinese in 1998 by Hebei Educational Press although it was the Western scholars who first "discovered" and then "rediscovered" this long-repressed Soviet-Russian thinker in the 1960s.

19   As far as the reception of postmodernism in China is concerned, I have published extensively both in Chinese and in English. In this respect, cf. my long essay, "The Mapping of Chinese Postmodernity", *Boundary 2: An International Journal of Literature and Culture* 24, no. 3 (1997): 19–40.

20   One of the exciting facts is that the Chinese government has decided to invest a huge amount of money to set up a dozen Chinese cultural centres in Western countries in an attempt to promote the Chinese language and culture worldwide.

CHAPTER 8 – TRANSLATION AS CULTURAL "DECOLONIZATION"

1   There are two conspicuous examples I would like to cite here: (1) the translation of the classical Chinese novel, *Honglou meng* (A Story of the Stone), by the British sinologist David Hawkes; and (2) the translation of the ancient English epic, *Beowulf,* by the Irish poet Seamus Heaney. Both have helped to popularize translations of recognized canonical literary works in a target language.

2   Paul Jay, "Beyond Discipline? Globalization and the Future of English", *PMLA* 116, no. 1 (January 2001): 33.

3   As for the former, the Chinese translation should be "Zhongguo wenxue", while the latter should be translated as "hanyu wenxue" or "huawen wenxue".

4   Homi Bhabha, ed., *Nation and Narration* (London: Routledge, 1990), "Introduction: Narrating the Nation", 4.

5   Although according to the rules of the International Olympic Committee, its members are not allowed to be invited to visit the cities bidding to host the Games, it is really a wonder that the Beijing Olympic Applying Committee translated all those documents into perfect English within a limited time. Even the spokesmen could express their views in fluent English, which, to my mind, certainly brought the two parties closer to each other. Most importantly, Mr. He Zhenliang expressed his ideas on behalf of the Chinese Delegation in both fluent English and French, which really moved the Committee members.

6   Homi Bhabha, *The Location of Culture* (New York: Routledge, 1994), 228.

7   Edward Said, "Globalizing Literary Study", *PMLA* 116, no. 1 (January 2001): 66.

8   It is interesting but ironic that while writing this chapter, my word processor indicated words like "decolonization", "postcolonialism" and

"postmodernity" as being incorrect, but accepted words like "kung fu" and "tofu" as being correct.

9   Gayatri C. Spivak, *A Critique of Postcolonial Reason: Toward a History of the Vanishing Present* (Cambridge, Massachusetts: Harvard University Press, 1999), 395.

10   Gayatri C. Spivak, "Moving Devi", *Cultural Critique* 47 (Winter 2001): 124.

CHAPTER 9 – CULTURAL STUDIES IN CHINA

1   Simon During, ed., introduction to *The Cultural Studies Reader* (London and New York: Routledge, 1993), 1.

2   *Ibid.*, 2.

3   As for the metamorphosed versions of postmodernism in the Chinese context, cf. Wang Ning, "The Reception of Postmodernism in China: The Case of Avant-Garde Fiction", in *International Postmodernism: Theory and Literary Practice*, eds. Hans Bertens and Douwe Fokkema (Amsterdam and Philadelphia: John Benjamins Company, 1997), 499–510; and Wang Ning, "The Mapping of Chinese Postmodernity", in *Postmodernism and China*, eds. Arif Dirlik and Xudong Zhang (Durham, NC: Duke University Press, 2000), 21–40. As for the practice of postcolonial criticism, it is even more complicated, for it is often associated with the revival of Neo-Confucianism and nationalism and the critique of Orientalism, with Zhang Yimou's and Chen Kaige's films as examples.

4   It is true that partly due to their ideas being similar to the official Chinese ideology and partly due to their personal relations with some Chinese scholars, Fredric Jameson and Terry Eagleton, two of the leading Marxist critics in the English-speaking world, are most frequently discussed and quoted in Chinese critical circles.

5   Cf. Wang Ning, "Dazhong wenhua he wenhua yanjiu" ("Popular Culture and Cultural Studies"), *Wenyi bao* (Literature and Art Gazette), 19 February 1994.

6   For instance, Qian Zhongwen, as co-editor of *Wenxue pinglun* (Literary Review), has published two of my essays and some others dealing with cultural studies and cultural identities with regard to globalization. Yue Daiyun, as co-editor of the series, *Kuawenhua duihua* (Cross-Cultural Dialogues), has published one essay of mine and many others concerning cultural studies.

7   Due to the fact that it is currently very difficult to register an official journal in China, *Wenhua yanjiu* was founded as a book series to be published yearly. But to our surprise, it is very popular among both literary scholars and cultural critics as well as ordinary young university students.

CHAPTER 10 – WHITMAN AND MODERNITY: TRANSLATION AND RECEPTION OF WHITMAN IN MODERN CHINESE LITERATURE

1 Malcom Bradbury and James McFarlane, eds., *Modernism: 1890–1930* (New York: Penguin Books, 1976), 43.

2 *Ibid.*, 243.

3 Cf. Gerald Graff, *Literature against Itself: Literary Ideas in Modern Society* (Chicago: University of Chicago Press, 1979), 58. Also cf. Ihab Hassan, *The Dismemberment of Orpheus: Toward a Postmodern Literature* (New York: Oxford University Press, 1971), especially pages 7, 8 and 252.

4 As for the critical and creative reception of Walt Whitman in China, cf. Fan Boqun and Zhu Donglin, eds., *1898–1949: Zhongwai wenxue bijiao shi* (A Comparative History of Chinese and Foreign Literatures: 1898–1949) (Nanjing: Jiangsu Education Press, 1993), 420–428. There is one section entitled "China's Whitman" which deals with Guo Moruo's reception of Whitman.

5 Cf. Douwe Fokkema, *Literary History, Modernism, and Postmodernism* (Amsterdam and Philadelphia: John Benjamins Publishing Company, 1984), 48.

6 As far as postmodernism or postmodernity as one of the different faces is concerned, cf. Matei Calinescu, *Five Faces of Modernity: Modernism, Avant-Garde, Decadence, Kitsch, Postmodernism* (Durham, NC: Duke University Press, 1987), especially his "Introduction".

7 Cf. Douwe Fokkema and Elrud Ibsch, *Modernist Conjectures: A Mainstream in European Literature 1910–1940* (London: Hurst and Company, 1987), 1–47.

8 Cf. James E. Miller, Jr., *A Critical Guide to* Leaves of Grass (Chicago: University of Chicago Press, 1957), especially 36–51.

9 As for the study of modern Chinese literature from a comparative perspective of influence and reception, cf. Yue Daiyun and Wang Ning, eds., *Xifang wenyisichao yu ershishiji zhongguowenxue* (Western Trends of Literary Thought and Twentieth-Century Chinese Literature) (Beijing: China Social Sciences Publishing House, 1990).

10 Cf. Jin Siyan, "Xinshi de qidai shiye" ("The Horizon of Expectation for New Chinese Poetry"), *ibid.*, 362.

11 Cf. Fan and Zhu, *1898–1949: Zhongwai wenxue bijiao shi*, 405–406.

12 Long Quanming, *Zhongguo xinshi liubian lun: 1917–1949* (On the Evolution of New Chinese Poetry: 1917–1949) (Beijing: People's Literature Press, 1999), 170.

13 Guo Moruo, "Xu wode shi" ("Preface to My Poetry"), in vol. 13 of *Moruo wenji* (Collected Works of Guo Moruo) (Beijing: People's Literature Press, 1959).

14 Guo Moruo, "Wode zuoshi de jingguo" ("The Process of My Writing of Poetry"), in vol. 11 of *Moruo wenji* (Collected Works of Guo Moruo) (Beijing: People's Literature Press, 1959), 143.

15 On Whitman's influence on Gu Cheng, cf. Liu Shusen's paper delivered at the international conference, Whitman 2000: American Poetry in a Global Context, which is entitled "Gu Cheng and Whitman: In Search of New Poetics". It was later published in Ed Folsom, ed., *Whitman East and West: New Contexts for Reading Walt Whitman* (Iowa City: University of Iowa Press, 2002), 208–220.

16 The two Chinese versions of *Leaves of Grass* were translated separately by Chu Tunan and Li Yeguang (published by the People's Literature Press, 1992) and Zhao Luorui (published by Shanghai Translation Press, 1996).

CHAPTER 11 – RECONSTRUCTING IBSEN AS AN ARTIST: TRANSLATION AND RECEPTION OF IBSEN IN CHINA

1 As far as the conferences held in the past few years are concerned, I will just mention a few important ones: The International Conference on Ibsen and Modernity in Regard to his Reception in China (26–28 June 1999, Beijing); The 9th International Ibsen Conference (5–10 June 2000, Bergen); Ibsen and Arts: Painting, Sculpture and Architecture Conference (24–27 October 2001, Rome); The International Conference on Ibsen and China: Toward an Aesthetic Construction (12–16 September 2002, Shanghai); The International Ibsen Conference and Theatre Festival: The Relevance of *A Doll's House*—Translation and Adaptation (8–14 November 2002, Dhaka).

2 In regard to the cultural translation and critical reception of Ibsen in China in the twentieth century, I would like to recommend the following three books: He Chengzhou's substantial study of the topic, which was first made as his PhD dissertation and then published in book form, entitled *Henrik Ibsen and Chinese Modern Drama* (Oslo: Unipub Forlag, 2002); Kwo-kan Tam's *Ibsen in China: 1908–1997* (Hong Kong: The Chinese University Press, 2001); and Wang Zhongxiang's *Yibusheng* (Ibsen) (Beijing: Huaxia Press, 2002, in Chinese). To me, all three have been written on the basis of the authors' close reading of Ibsen's original works or with the help of the English translation of his works, and represent the state of the art of Ibsen studies in China.

3 Cf. Wang Ning, "Multiple Codes in Ibsen's Drama", in *Ibsen Research Papers*, eds. Meng Shengde et al. (Beijing: Chinese Literature Press), 271.

4 Jameson gave his speech on modernity on 31 July 2002 at the Chinese Academy of Social Sciences, Beijing.

5 Cf. Ibsen's letter to his publisher on 16 March 1882, in Einar Haugen, *Ibsen's Drama: Author to Audience* (Minneapolis: University of Minnesota Press, 1979), 3.

6 I should particularly point out here that, inspired by Ibsen's artistic imagination, some Chinese directors, such as Wu Xiaojiang and Sun Huizhu, have retranslated Ibsen's plays, such as *A Doll's House*, *Heddar Gabler*, *Ghosts*, and *Peer Gynt*, and restaged them in the postmodern society, thus making these old canonical works significant in contemporary China. Cf. Douwe Fokkema and Elrud Ibsch, *Modernist Conjectures: A Mainstream*

in European Literature 1910–1940 (London: Hurst and Company, 1987), 1–47.

7   Malcom Bradbury and James McFarlane, eds., *Modernism: 1890–1930* (New York: Penguin Books, 1976), 499.

8   As for studies of Ibsen's plays from the postmodern perspective, cf. Charles R. Lyons, "Ibsen's Realism and the Predicates of Postmodernism", *Contemporary Approaches to Ibsen* 8 (1994): 185–204; Wang Ning, "Postmodernizing Ibsen: Toward a New Interpretation of the Fin-de-Siecle", in *Ibsen im europaischen Spannungsfeld zwischen Naturalismus und Symbolismus*, eds. Maria Deppermann et al. (Frankfurt am Main: Peter Lang, 1998), 295–307.

9   Haugen, *Ibsen's Drama: Author to Audience*, 74.

10   *Ibid.*, 3–4.

11   Cf. Brian Johnston, *Text and Supertext in Ibsen's Drama* (London: The Pennsylvania State University Press, 1989), 7.

12   *Ibid.*, 9–27.

13   I should point out with pleasure that at two recent international conferences on Ibsen held in China, most of the Chinese participants were already able to discuss with their international colleagues directly in English so that equitable dialogues could be carried out without simultaneous interpretations. But in the past, almost all the Ibsen scholars in China were either from the Chinese department or from the department of theatre, in which a high English proficiency was not required.

14   Cf. Jean-Francois Lyotard, *The Postmodern Condition: A Report on Knowledge*, trans. Geoff Bennington and Brian Massumi (Minneapolis: University of Minnesota Press, 1984), 81.

15   Perhaps due to the fact that such important May 4th intellectual leaders as Lu Xun and Hu Shi were involved in introducing and translating Ibsen in the Chinese context, Ibsen was regarded more as a revolutionary thinker than as a dramatist.

16   In this special issue on Ibsen, it is particularly worth reading Hu Shi's long article entitled "Yibusheng zhuyi" ("Ibsenism"), *Xin Qingnian* (New Youth) 4, no. 6 (1918): 489–507.

17   As for the study of modern Chinese literature from a comparative perspective of influence and reception, cf. Yue Daiyun and Wang Ning, eds., *Xifang wenyisichao yu ershishiji zhongguowenxue* (Western Trends of Literary Thought and Twentieth-Century Chinese Literature) (Beijing: China Social Sciences Publishing House, 1990).

18   It is true that in recent years, great advances have been made in China's Ibsen studies largely because of the rise of a group of young scholars who are able to write or present their papers directly in English. For instance, on such occasions as in the International Conference on Ibsen and Modernity in Regard to his Reception in China (26–28 June 1999, Beijing) and the International Conference on Ibsen and China: Toward an Aesthetic Construction (12–16 September 2002, Shanghai), most of the Chinese participants were able to carry out dialogues with the international participants in English.

Index

Other Titles on Cultural Studies

Militancy and Religion
by Ban Kah Choon
ISBN 981 210 313 9

The Boat and the City: Chinese Diaspora and the Architecture of Southeast Asian Coastal Cities
by Johannes Widodo
ISBN 981 210 253 1

Dismantling Time: Chinese Literature in the Age of Globalization
by Lu Jie
ISBN 981 210 288 4

Cultural Studies in China
edited by Jin Yuanpu and Tao Dongfeng
ISBN 981 210 289 2

Religious Studies in China
edited by Yang Huilin
ISBN 981 210 292 2

Studies of Literature and Arts in China
edited by Fang Ning
ISBN 981 210 291 4

Globalization and China
by Wang Ning
ISBN 981 210 282 5

In Search of the Chinese Self-Identity
by Chen Yongguo
ISBN 981 210 285 X

English and the Experience of Modernity
edited by Ban Kah Choon and Hu Zhuanglin
ISBN 981 210 283 3

Translating China
by Luo Xuanmin
ISBN 981 210 286 8

The Business of China
edited by Xiao Guanglin and Shi Anbin
ISBN 981 210 287 6

Mediating *Chineseness*: Identity Politics and Media Culture in Contemporary China
by Shi Anbin
ISBN 981 210 421 6

Multinational Corporations' Public Relations in China: An Interpretive Study of Public Relations Culture
by Liu Xi
ISBN 981 210 422 4

For more information on pricing and availability, please log on to
www.marshallcavendish.com/academic